P9-BJM-404

CAMROSE LUTHERAN COLLEGE
LIBRARY

FAMILY VIOLENCE: EMERGING ISSUES OF A NATIONAL CRISIS

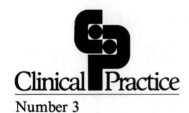

Clinical Practice
Number 3

Judith H. Gold, M.D., F.R.C.P.(C)
Series Editor

FAMILY VIOLENCE: EMERGING ISSUES OF A NATIONAL CRISIS

Edited by

LEAH J. DICKSTEIN, M.D.

Professor, Department of Psychiatry and Behavioral Sciences, and Associate Dean for Student Affairs (School of Medicine); Psychiatric Consultant, Counseling Center, University of Louisville, Kentucky

CAROL C. NADELSON, M.D.

Professor and Vice-Chair and Director of Education and Training, Department of Psychiatry, Tufts–New England Medical Center, Boston, Massachusetts; Immediate Past President, American Psychiatric Association

1400 K Street, N.W.
Washington, DC 20005

Note: The authors have worked to ensure that all information in this book concerning drug dosages, schedules, and routes of administration is accurate at the time of publication and consistent with standards set by the U.S. Food and Drug Administration and the general medical community. As medical research and practice advance, however, therapeutic standards may change. For this reason and because human and mechanical errors sometimes occur, we recommend that readers follow the advice of a physician directly involved in their care or the care of a member of their family.

Books published by American Psychiatric Press, Inc. represent the views and opinions of the individual authors and do not necessarily reflect the policies and opinions of the Press or the American Psychiatric Association.

Copyright © 1989 American Psychiatric Press, Inc.
All Rights Reserved
92 91 90 89 88 5 4 3 2 1

Manufactured in the U.S.A.

The paper used in this publication meets the minimum requirements of American National Standard for Information Sciences—Permanence of Paper for Printed Library Materials ANSI Z39.48-1984. ♾

Library of Congress Cataloging-in-Publication Data

Family violence: emerging issues of a national crisis / edited by Leah J. Dickstein and Carol C. Nadelson.
    p.   cm.—(Clinical practice series; no. 3)
  Based on a symposium held during the 1986 American Psychiatric Association Annual Meeting in Washington, D.C.
  Bibliography: p.
  ISBN 0-88048-146-3
  1. Family violence—United States—Congresses. 2. Family violence—United States—Prevention—Congresses. 3. Abused wives—United States—Congresses. I. Dickstein, Leah J., 1934– . II. Nadelson, Carol C. III. American Psychiatric Association. Meeting (139th: 1986: Washington, D.C.) IV. Series.
  [DNLM: 1. Family—United States—congresses. 2. Violence—United States—congresses. HQ 809.3.U5 F198 1986]
HQ809.3.U5F34 1987
362.8′2—dc 19
DNLM/DLC
for Library of Congress

87-30806
CIP

65399

HQ
809.3
.U5
F34
1989

Contents

CAMROSE LUTHERAN COLLEGE
LIBRARY

Contributors

David Adams, M.Ed., C.A.G.S, L.C.S.W.
Director, Emerge, A Men's Counseling Service on Domestic Violence, Boston, Massachusetts

Elissa P. Benedek, M.D.
Director, Research and Training, Center for Forensic Psychiatry, Ann Arbor, Michigan

Elaine Carmen, M.D.
Professor of Psychiatry, Boston University School of Medicine; Clinical Director, Crisis Intervention Unit, The Dr. Solomon Carter Fuller Mental Health Center, Boston, Massachusetts

John R. Conte, M.D.
Assistant Professor, School of Social Service Administration, University of Chicago, Illinois

Leah J. Dickstein, M.D.
Professor, Department of Psychiatry and Behavioral Sciences and Associate Dean for Student Affairs (School of Medicine), and Psychiatric Consultant (Counseling Center), University of Louisville, Kentucky

Marion Zucker Goldstein, M.D.
Assistant Clinical Professor and Director, Division of Geriatric Psychiatry, State University of New York at Buffalo

Judith Herman, M.D.
Assistant Clinical Professor, Department of Psychiatry, Cambridge Hospital, Harvard Medical School, Boston; Member of Women's Mental Health Collective, A Woman-Controlled Clinic in Somerville, Massachusetts

Lisa G. Lerman, J.D., LL.M.
Attorney, Washington, D.C.

Howard B. Levy, M.D.
Chair, Department of Pediatrics, Mount Sinai Hospital
Medical Center; Associate Professor of Pediatrics, Rush
Medical College, Chicago, Illinois

Mary Lystad, Ph.D.
Chief, Emergency Services Branch, National Institute of
Mental Health, Rockville, Maryland

Peter J. Mancuso, Jr.
Assistant Director of Training, New York City Police
Academy

Carol C. Nadelson, M.D.
Professor and Vice-Chair and Director of Education and
Training, Department of Psychiatry, Tufts–New England
Medical Center, Boston, Massachusetts; Past President,
American Psychiatric Association

Marla Sauzier, M.D.
Clinical Instructor in Psychiatry, Harvard Medical School,
Boston, Massachusetts

Stephen H. Sheldon, D.O.
Director, Division of Educational Research and
Development, Department of Pediatrics, Mount Sinai
Hospital; Assistant Professor of Pediatrics and Preventative
Medicine, Rush Medical College, Chicago, Illinois

Deborah Williams-White
Information and Advocacy Coordinator, National Coalition
Against Domestic Violence, Washington, D.C.

Introduction
to the Clinical Practice Series

Over the years of its existence the series of monographs entitled *Clinical Insights* gradually became focused on providing current, factual, and theoretical material of interest to the clinician working outside of a hospital setting. To reflect this orientation, the name of the Series has been changed to *Clinical Practice*.

The Clinical Practice Series will provide readers with books that give the mental health clinician a practical clinical approach to a variety of psychiatric problems. These books will provide up-to-date literature reviews and emphasize the most recent treatment methods. Thus, the publications in the Series will interest clinicians working both in psychiatry and in the other mental health professions.

Each year a number of books will be published dealing with all aspects of clinical practice. In addition, from time to time when appropriate, the publications may be revised and updated. Thus, the Series will provide quick access to relevant and important areas of psychiatric practice. Some books in the Series will be authored by a person considered to be an expert in that particular area; others will be edited by such an expert who will also draw together other knowledgeable authors to produce a comprehensive overview of that topic.

Some of the books in the Clinical Practice Series will have their foundation in presentations at an Annual Meeting of the American Psychiatric Association. All will contain the most recently available information on the subjects discussed. Theoretical and scientific data will be applied to clinical situations, and case illustrations will be utilized in order to make the material even more relevant for the practitioner. Thus, the Clinical Practice Series should provide educational reading in a compact format especially written for the mental health clinician–psychiatrist.

Violence occurring within families is a subject that is ignored often by professionals and by the public despite its alarming frequency. Family violence, as you will read, involves as its victims, children, spouses, especially women, and the elderly. All those working in psychiatry should not only be acutely aware of the frequency of violence and abuse within families, but also train themselves to be alert for it in those they are treating. This book offers treatment approaches as well as broad discussions of all aspects of family violence.

Judith H. Gold, M.D., F.R.C.P.(C)
Series Editor,
Clinical Practice Series

Introduction

I never thought of it as violence because I never really took her seriously, like she was a piece of furniture. At Emerge, I've learned to respect my wife. It took some time for it to sink in but I see now how I was keeping her back, not just with my violence, but with all the other ways I had of putting her down.

—former client,
Emerge newsletter,
A Men's Counseling Service on Domestic Violence

*T*his monograph is an outgrowth of a presidential public symposium entitled "Family Violence" that took place during the 1986 American Psychiatric Association (APA) annual meeting in Washington, D.C. Carol C. Nadelson, M.D., completing her tenure as first woman president of the APA, had decided that the topic of family violence was a major national priority and therefore chose to invite the public to join national and local experts in discussion.

The participants included Leah J. Dickstein, M.D., chair; Carol C. Nadelson, M.D., co-chair; Robert W. Gibson, M.D., co-chair; Elaine Carmen, M.D.; Deborah Williams-White; David Adams, M.Ed., L.C.S.W.; Lisa G. Lerman, J.D., LL.M.; Mary Lystad, Ph.D.; and Elissa P. Benedek, M.D., discussant. Robert W. Gibson, M.D., President and Chief Executive Officer of Sheppard Pratt Hospital in Baltimore, Maryland, represented his institution, which generously supported the symposium.

This edited volume, directed toward health and mental health professionals, is based on the symposium. Additional chapters were included to ensure that all major aspects of the topic are explored.

Family violence is not a new problem; in fact, it is probably as old as humankind and has been documented back to Biblical times. In the United States, spouse and child abuse arrived with the Puritans, but public outcry began as an active movement in 1973. Ironically, although the sequence of recognition of abused victims began first with children and then expanded to include focus on adult victims, only most recently has the focus shifted to the origin of the problem—that is, the family structure as the major setting for personal abuse.

Not surprisingly, we find discrepancies in the incidence and prevalence statistics cited in several chapters. However, if we note the difference in the dates when the research was published, then these variations simply reflect more available and refined data as well as less reticence on the victims' part to acknowledge and share their traumas. In addition, for the past decade, more public and professional attention has been focused on the recognition of family violence. Child abuse became a mandatory reportable occurrence in the United States in 1968. In 1985 elder abuse was added to federal statutes as H.R. 1674. Consequently, today more people who previously had suffered in silence and fear, thinking themselves helpless to stop abuse and not knowing where to turn or what to do, can seek advice, support, and protection.

Denial exists on the part of individuals and society, and the problems of family violence continue to be minimized among victims, abusers, and professionals. Even among mental health professionals, family violence may be unrecognized, misunderstood, and, unfortunately, ignored. Clearly what must be unconditionally accepted is that *family violence of some kind currently occurs in half the homes in the United States at least once a year.*

By definition family violence occurs in physical, emotional, and psychological form and includes child abuse, sibling abuse, spouse abuse, homicide, abuse of elderly parents by their adult children, abuse of middle-aged adults by their adolescent children, and abuse of handicapped family members.

Women, in their roles as wives and significant others, represent the largest number of victims of abuse and batterings. In fact, it is not uncommon that more than one type of family violence occurs in a home. Researchers have indicated not only that *violence is a learned behavior*, but unfortunately that this learning usually occurs in the home. While we often idealize the family home as a place of love and refuge, it must now also be thought of as a training ground for violence.

Dr. Elissa Benedek, in her opening chapter, provides us with a context, description, and perspective on victims as well as abusing families. She provides salient preventive strategies and exhorts us to attend actively to this human blight.

In Chapter 2, Dr. Elaine Carmen summarizes her research into the psychosocial consequences of abuse for victims and offers important perspectives on how the victim becomes a patient. She emphasizes the pervasiveness of the problem and delineates the role of psychiatrists in treating victims.

Known risk factors in the occurrence of father–daughter incest as well as common characteristics and defense mechanisms of abusive and silent parents and child victims are described by Dr. Judith Herman in Chapter 3. Specific alternatives at the various treatment stages of father—daughter incest are outlined along with an important discussion of the need for restoration of a constructive mother–daughter relationship.

Spouse abuse is discussed by Ms. Deborah Williams-White in Chapter 4. Whether or not they are legally married, abused women face multiple problems and may need multiple approaches to gain control, once more, over their lives. Ms. Williams-White provides specific guidelines for the different professionals who may interact with these women: hospital personnel, physicians, mental health professionals, police officers and other members of the criminal justice system, as well as social service workers and educators.

A unique orientation and treatment program based on his work with male abusers is detailed by Mr. David Adams in

Chapter 5. His most important emphasis is on anti-sexist education for the abusers. He has found that this can promote constructive psychological change in self-awareness and social awareness and consequent cessation of abuse. The issues of power and control are seen as central to the men's stereotypic and negative attitudes toward the women they abuse. Through individual and group therapy the men gain an understanding of their problems, and they change their attitudes and behavior. Mr. Adams's vivid vignettes highlight his effective program.

Dr. Marion Zucker Goldstein, in Chapter 6, poignantly introduces the topic of elder abuse and summarizes basic issues as well as recent government policies regarding this growing victim population. She skillfully presents the dilemmas for the victim, the victimizer, and the various agencies that are assigned the task of developing constructive solutions.

In Chapter 7, Mr. Peter Mancuso offers insights into the theory, policy, and practice patterns involved in dealing with family violence that the New York City police department has developed over the past 20 years. This clear and detailed information should go a long way toward enabling mental health and other professionals to work more constructively and rationally with the police system regarding family violence.

In Chapter 8, Ms. Lisa Lerman emphasizes an area that has long been ignored—the role of mental health professionals in stopping abuse. She emphasizes a law-enforcement-oriented response, rather than a conciliation-oriented response, on the part of the mental health professional, who is often the only or primary professional in contact with the abuser and the victim.

Drs. Carol Nadelson and Maria Sauzier in Chapter 9 discuss the epidemiology and demographics, as well as common life experiences and interactions, of male abusers and female victims. A model program for sexually abused children and their families, called the Family Crisis Program, is described. Details from the program's conceptual basis to countertransference issues, as well as the multiplicity of necessary services needed in such a program, are outlined.

In Chapter 10, Drs. Howard Levy, Stephen Sheldon, and John Conte, using a systems approach, describe current difficulties in the ways in which various community agencies and professionals interact to serve child victims of family violence. They propose changes not only in programs, but also in professionals' attitudes toward the recognition, treatment, and prevention of abuse. In addition, they offer useful tables of vulnerability factors in the children, parents, and environment of family violence and emphasize the initial need for interdisciplinary research.

In the final chapter, Dr. Mary Lystad outlines and discusses psychosocial and cultural causes of family violence and then presents a series of proposed community intervention–prevention programs. These programs address individuals at high risk, such as teenagers, before they assume their own family leadership roles. Additionally, outreach programs directed to families with unique stressors, the social system (including teachers), the workplace, the justice system, and the mass media are included. Perhaps the most cogent statement made by Dr. Lystad is that the public must assume responsibility now for action to be taken currently and in the future to decrease this crisis of unrecognized proportions and untold repercussions.

We dedicate this book to all those who have experienced family violence. We hope other professionals will add to the information contained in these chapters, through research and innovative educational programs, so that families may function free of the pain, fear, and tragedy that are currently part of our national epidemic of family violence.

Leah J. Dickstein, M.D.
Carol C. Nadelson, M.D.

Acknowledgments

To the staff of the American Psychiatric Press, Inc., we offer gratitude for assistance in the process of completing this book. We want to acknowledge the help of many secretaries and assistants to all the authors. However, we especially want to recognize five women at the University of Louisville School of Medicine: Jayne Zickafoose, Kathy Garvin, Leslie Key-Pfister, Kim Mayes, and Lillian Jones. These individuals contacted all of the contributors for the original symposium and for this book over the past two and a half years and typed and retyped all the chapters with skill and good cheer. Finally, on behalf of all who read this book, we want to acknowledge and express our sincere appreciation for the extraordinary efforts expended by our colleagues who made time to research and share their knowledge in these insightful chapters.

Baseball, Apple Pie, and Violence: Is It American?

ELISSA P. BENEDEK, M.D.

Chapter 1

Baseball, Apple Pie, and Violence: Is It American?

Violent behavior in America is at an all-time high and seems to be increasing. We are a violent society. Each day new and more spectacular violent acts are reported in the media. In the past we believed that violent acts were more common among the poor, urban, young male minorities, school dropouts, persons from broken homes, and emotionally disturbed slum dwellers. We believed that violent acts were more common among "them," not us. We now know that violent acts can be located in any home in America, in any part of an American city, in a ghetto or in a suburban affluent neighborhood. We now know that violence is an epidemic. The level of violence in our society is so high that we can no longer ignore it. However, our ignorance in regard to causes, prevention, and treatment is vast.

As a psychiatrist working in a forensic mental health center, my daily clinical life is filled with victims of violence and their victimizers. As a person, I abhor violence. As a clinician, I also abhor violence. Despite the fact that the identification, evaluation, and treatment of violent individuals are a major part of my professional life, I have never become inured or desensitized to it. In this chapter I shall present brief vignettes of the multiple clinical appearances of violent behavior in family life, comment briefly on the common characteristics of families where violent behavior occurs, and finally, suggest strategies for prevention, identification, treatment, and research as they apply to violent patients, their families, and their communities.

3

Clinical Examples of Domestic Violence

Domestic Violence

Mary C., a 32-year-old black woman, was evaluated at the Forensic Center after the murder of her 40-year-old Hispanic lover. Mary and her lover had lived together intermittently for 12 years. He had fathered all of her four children. He was the last man whom Mary lived with, but since the age of 16 she had lived with three other men who supported her economically yet destroyed her emotionally. Her last lover, James, abused alcohol. However, alcohol abuse was not solely responsible for the many beatings James inflicted. He beat Mary when he was drunk or sober, angry or happy, employed or unemployed. His beatings were predictably unpredictable. Mary left home with her four children on numerous occasions, but her relatives were no longer able or willing to provide shelter for her. Police had been called to Mary's home frequently and now responded to her calls slowly and impatiently. On the night of the murder, Mary had been held against a hot radiator by her boyfriend. Deep burns were present and painful. Mary had fled across the street to her sister's home and had managed to call the police from there once again. The police arrived and were standing at Mary's side when she picked up a kitchen knife and stabbed and killed her lover. Mary explained that she had, as she perceived it, no choice. She had previously exhausted all other lawful remedies and now believed it was "either her lover or herself." She believed prison would be preferable to "hell on earth." Tragically, Mary had never had any social service contacts or mental health counseling.

Rape

Charles C., a 16-year-old boy, lost his father at an early age and was raised by his mother and aunts. At age 14 Charles met a man at a gas station who gave him a job and became a friend and substitute father. Charles's new father indoctrinated him in anal homosexual behavior, explaining to Charles that anal sex would increase his manhood. When Charles's mother became concerned, Charles was coerced psychologically into accompanying the man on a cross-country trip during which he was regularly beaten and sexually abused. Charles was identified as a missing child when an alert employer noted the picture of a boy who resembled Charles on a milk carton, with these boldly printed words: "Missing, Please Help Find this Boy." Charles's mother, a middle-class, well-educated woman, was unaware of programs in her community for young boys until after tragedy and violence in the form of sexual abuse struck her home.

Elder Abuse

Ronald S., a 75-year-old man, had lived and raised a family in a middle-class, urban neighborhood. Ronald's nuclear family then moved away; he remained and lived alone. Ronald was regularly teased and taunted by the neighborhood children, who also vandalized his home. Ronald alleged that he kept a rifle on the premises for protection in an attempt to scare the neighborhood vandals and to prevent their constant harassment. Ronald shot and accidentally killed a 12-year-old child.

Statistics

Domestic violence, spouse abuse, child abuse, child sexual abuse, and elder abuse are the more common manifestations of violence in our communities today. The Department of Justice reported that there were at least 4.1 million cases of family violence between 1973 and 1981, or an average of 450,000 per year (Department of Justice 1984). The department added, in its "Special Report on Family Violence," that the reported figure "was probably significantly lower than the actual number of cases since these estimates reflect only behavior that victims are willing to label as criminal and report to survey interviewers" (Department of Justice 1984). Steven Sleshinger, Director of the Bureau of Justice Statistics, pointed out,

5

It is striking that the national crime survey uncovers about 450,000 cases of family violence each year through a technique that was originally designed to measure such crimes as burglary, robbery, larceny, and aggravated assault. Undoubtedly, many more cases are not reported to either police or survey interviewers because victims do not recognize the abuse as criminal, they feel too much shame to report it, or they feel hopeless about the possibility of stopping it.

The report included the following important conclusion:

Considering that over a nine year period there have been 4.1 million victimizations committed by relatives reported to a government agency and that a substantial number of these occurred at least three times during a six-month period, it is apparent that family violence is a significant problem of large and currently ill-understood proportions.

All researchers who work in the area of family violence agree that family violence is underreported. Victims of violence are reluctant to reveal the etiology of their injuries either to medical personnel or to the criminal justice system. The few statistics and trends we note are horrifying. For example, a person is considerably more likely to be killed by a member of his or her own family than by a stranger. Domestic disturbance is the most common call received by police. It has been estimated that between 30 to 50 percent of all marriages will at some point involve the use of physical violence and that annually as many as two million children may be physically abused by their parents. All forms of violence considered, it is estimated that between five and six million children, spouses, and elderly individuals are neglected, battered, and abused in the United States every year (National Clearing House on Justice Reference Service 1984).

In regard to the incidence and prevalence of child sexual abuse, although statistics are unclear, reports reveal that about one-fifth to one-third of adult women have had a childhood sexual encounter with an adult male and about one percent of adult women have had a sexual experience with a father or stepfather (Herman 1981; Finkelhor 1979, 1980). In regard to adult males, Landis (1956) reported that approximately 30 percent of a sample of 500 university students who admitted that they were child victims of sexual abuse were male.

Characteristics of Abusive Families

Certain common characteristics are found in violent families, although individual families may not fit the mold or model. It has been widely asserted that *abusive families tend to be isolated* both from family support and the support of community organizations. Kempe et al. (1983) report that abusive families lack "a life line." This is to say, they have no external connection, supports, or models. In addition, social isolation begets social isolation so that parents and children in abusive families are enmeshed. Consequently, children have no opportunity to observe or model other methods of family interaction.

Alcohol or drug abuse may be prevalent in the abusive family but is not a necessary component of violence. Alcohol or drugs may serve as an excuse to allow a violent person a rationale for disinhibition or dyscontrol. Alcohol or drugs are physiologic disinhibitors that lower frustration tolerance and inhibition of aggressive impulses. Controlled substances may impair thinking, judgment, and reality testing and allow behavior to take precedence over cognitive methods of problem solving.

Unemployment and economic deprivation serve as additional stressors in all forms of family violence. The statistical correlation between national periods of unemployment and the increase in family violence, particularly child abuse, is clear. With unemployment, more people may be crowded into the family home and less psychologic and physical space exists. Boundaries often become blurred. With more contact there is more opportunity for conflict. Violence is much more likely to occur in families experiencing unemployment. Unemployment in the work force is significantly related to child abuse. In addition to unemployment, there appears to be a relationship between *job dissatisfaction*, child mistreatment, and domestic violence.

The Victim

Victims of violence have often been exposed to violence in their families of origin. They may have witnessed marital violence or been psychologically or physically abused as children. Experts agree that violence breeds more violence and there is an intergenerational cycle of violence. This association seems to be, for the most part, environmental rather than genetic in nature.

Victims of violence are most often related. A victim may have a special meaning in the family and be identified as a family scapegoat. A victim may be special because of a physical handicap or an emotional disorder. Furthermore, a victim may occupy a unique position in the family, for example, as the oldest or the youngest. Victims frequently are repeatedly revictimized. That is to say, the victim of childhood abuse may become the abused spouse or sexually assaulted spouse. Carmen and Rieker (1984) note that "Victims blame themselves as they come to believe that the abuse can only be explained by their essential badness." They suggest that abused patients accept the reality of their abusers, who believe that the victims are bad and deserve the abuse. Thus, the victims come to expect abuse from many interpersonal relationships.

Strategies for Prevention

A Presidential Commission studied mental retardation in part because of the publicity given and concern voiced in relation to President Kennedy's retarded sister. Clinicians working in the area of violence have often joked that they hoped a President and his or her family might have personal contact with violence. Although no one has suggested that the assassination attempt on President Reagan prompted a Surgeon General's Workshop on Violence and Public Health, the two may possibly be correlated. The workshop produced a report that dealt with diverse forms of violence in terms of policy evaluation, treatment, and research recommendations (Surgeon General's Workshop on Violence and Public Health 1985). The policy recommendations are interesting and somewhat novel. The report recommends that

1. There should be a complete and universal federal ban on the sale, manufacture, importation, and possession of handguns except for authorized police and military personnel; and regulations on the manufacture, sale, and distribution of other lethal weapons such as martial arts items (for example, numb chuck stars and knives).

   A ban on handguns would do much to reduce violence in our homes and streets. The availability of a weapon in times of crisis clearly contributes to violent behavior.

2. There should be criminal penalties associated with possession of any weapon where alcohol is sold or served.

   Earlier in this chapter, comments were made about the clear association of alcohol and illegal substances with all forms of violence. Unquestionably, chemical and psychologic effects of alcohol and drugs are intertwined. Actual and perceived disinhibition of aggressive impulses leads to a clear association of alcohol with all violent crime.

3. There should be development and implementation of a full employment policy for the nation with immediate attention aimed at the creation of jobs for those at high risk as either abusers or victims. Identifying who is at high risk as an abuser will be difficult, but not impossible. We know that young men who have been involved in

criminal behavior are more likely to progress to violent activities.

4. There should be an aggressive government policy to reduce racial discrimination and sexism.

5. There should be a decrease in the cultural acceptance of violence by discouraging corporal punishment in the home, forbidding corporal punishment in the school, and abolishing capital punishment by the state because all are models and sanctions of violence. Cultural acceptance of violence in our society not only condones violent behavior but provides role models for it. The progression of learning is obvious: The state provides a model for the family, the family provides a model for the child. Capital punishment and state-supported corporal punishment in the schools convey implicit and explicit messages to families.

6. There should be a decrease in the portrayal of violence on television and discouragement of the presentation of violent role models in all media forms, with encouragement of the presentation of positive, nonviolent role models. Television has a role in antisocial and prosocial behavior. It is unclear, however, whether media portrayal of violence only influences those individuals who are otherwise at risk or creates risk in itself. Nevertheless, the portrayal of violence as a legitimate method of interaction or means to achieve a goal clearly has early effects on developing children.

7. The public should be made aware that alcohol consumption may be hazardous to health because of its association with violence.

8. Research must be conducted concerning the possible relationships between our policy of deinstitutionalization and the current lack of adequate community-based support services for the mentally ill and their families, with known rates of assaultive violence and victimization.

Violent behavior among the mentally ill seems to

be increasing as the lack of community and social supports for these patients also increases. We have noted earlier that violence is often the last cry for help when other methods seem futile. Currently it appears that the mentally ill have fewer and fewer resources available to them. In some mentally ill patients, violence serves to reinstitutionalize them either in hospitals or prisons and jails and thus provides obvious external control for their internal problems. Reinstitutionalization itself may also have contributed to this increase in violent behavior.

9. Communication and cooperation should be promoted between health care providers, criminal justice agencies, schools, and social service agencies to improve the identification of early intervention techniques and the treatment of high-risk individuals.
10. Communities should have health care facilities with comprehensive multidisciplinary programs that address the detection, assessment, and treatment of all forms of interpersonal violence for victims, perpetrators, and their families. Particular attention should be given to the detection of and intervention for persons known to be at high risk.
11. We should encourage health education demonstration projects for the family, school, and community aimed at decreasing interpersonal violence. These projects should be evaluated for their effectiveness, efficacy, and replicability.

The working group for the Surgeon General's Workshop recognized the importance of experimental and demonstration projects as important ways of encouraging the development of novel approaches. These projects need to be evaluated not only for their effectiveness, efficacy, and replicability, but also for their ethical and legal implications. Unfortunately, certain projects in the past, designed to reduce violence, have had problematic, ethical, or legal implications that were only uncovered during the duration of the project:

essentially these projects revictimized already victimized populations.

12. The education of health professionals should include training in the identification, treatment, and/or referral of victims, perpetrators, and persons at high risk for violence.

These overarching suggestions were made in regard to the detection, evaluation, and treatment of victims of modern day violence in America and are detailed in the Report.

Conclusion

In "A Modest Proposal to Reduce Violence in America," Clark (1981) reminds us that there are

> many forms of violence. . . . Foremost is war and its threat that violence is supreme and slaughters millions and insurrection and terrorism are politically motivated violence that cannot be ignored. Poverty, with its forms of starvation, malnutrition, sickness, ignorance and want is a form of violence as deadly as gunfire.

Clark concluded his modest proposals by suggesting,

> By commitment and conduct we must make gentleness a virtue. We must see violence as the ultimate human degradation. Disputes should be resolved by reason, by compassion, by democratic process. Freedom and equality should be our practice as they are our preachment. Violence must be recognized as the ultimate despot driving us to force and violence.

It is only through constant vigilance and attention to precursors of violence in ourselves, in our families, and in our communities that we can hope to begin social policies of primary prevention. We cannot hope to end global violence until we decrease the violence in ourselves and our own homes, backyards, and neighborhoods.

References

Carmen EC, Rieker PP, Mills T: Victims of violence and psychiatric illness. Am J Psychiatry 141:378-383, 1984

Clark R: A modest proposal to reduce violence in America, in Violence and the Violent Individual. Edited by Hays JR, Roberts TK, Solway KS. New York, SP Medical and Scientific Books, 1981

Department of Justice: Special Report on Family Violence. April 22, 1984

Finkelhor D: Sexually Victimized Children. New York, Free Press, 1979

Finkelhor D: Risk factors in the sexual victimization of children. Child Abuse and Neglect 265, 1980

Herman J: Father–Daughter Incest. Cambridge, MA, Harvard University Press, 1981

Kempe N, Meichenbaum DH, Jaremko M (eds): Stress Reduction and Prevention. New York, Plenum, 1983

Landis JT: Experiences of 500 children with adult sexual deviations. Psychiatr Q (suppl) 30:91, 1956

National Clearing House on Justice Reference Service: Family Violence, 1984

Surgeon General's Workshop on Violence and Public Health: Recommendations for the working group (Unpublished report), October 1985

Chapter 2

Family Violence and the Victim-to-Patient Process

ELAINE CARMEN, M.D.

Chapter 2

Family Violence and the Victim-to-Patient Process

*I*n the last 15 years, there has been heightened public awareness of the problem of violence in general, violence in families, and violence against women. As a consequence, we have seen the emergence of a highly influential victims' rights and victim assistance movement along with the passage of federal legislation designed for victim relief. In 1985, for example, the Surgeon General announced his intention to mount an aggressive educational and prevention campaign against violence and family violence as major public health problems. We owe much of this awareness to the successful efforts of the women's movement to highlight the endemic nature of rape, wife beating, and child sexual abuse in our culture.

Indeed, it is in the body of work on victimization of women—rape, incest, and wife abuse—that the most extensive reformulation of traditional psychologic theories of women's pain and suffering has occurred (Rieker and Carmen 1986). In sharp contrast to the most prevalent psychologic explanations that locate the problem within the victim—for example, masochism—violence against women is more accurately conceptualized as one of the most destructive consequences of the sexual inequality in existing social institutions (Hilberman 1980). What else besides inequality could explain the fact that women and children are the most vulnerable targets of violence in families and of all forms of sexual abuse?

17

This chapter, then, is about the victims of family violence—women and children. After commenting briefly on the prevalence of victimization, I summarize my research into the psychosocial consequences of abuse for victims (Carmen et al. 1984) and, finally, offer some perspectives on the victim-to-patient process and the role of psychiatrists in treating victims (Rieker and Carmen 1986).

Prevalence

Family violence occurs in every social class and every racial, cultural, ethnic, religious, and educational group. Some of these families are highly disorganized, and some appear to be in no way out of the ordinary or deviant. Physical and sexual abuse are frequent, if not inevitable, life experiences for many people. In a random sample of adult women, Russell found that 38 percent had been sexually abused before age 18; 16 percent had been abused by family members (1984). Women in this country stand a 1 in 4 chance of being raped (Russell 1982); 1 woman in 3 and 1 man in 10 are sexually molested in childhood (Finkelhor 1979); countless numbers of children are abused by parents and other intimates, and women are beaten and raped by their husbands.

It is estimated that 25 percent of adult women in the United States have been physically abused at least once by a male intimate. Spouse abuse may be the single most common etiology for injuries presented by women to health care providers. Estimates are that 25 percent of females seen by psychiatric emergency services have histories of domestic violence; 25 percent of obstetrical patients are in abusive relationships; and 40 to 50 percent of all female alcohol-related problems seen in emergency medical and psychiatric services may be precipitated by abuse (Stark and Flitcraft 1985). Families in which women are abused are also families in which children are at high risk for physical and sexual abuse.

Abuse and Psychiatric Illness: Research Findings

Despite the large numbers of victims of family violence, mental health professionals remain generally unaware of the social and psychological consequences of abuse—and there are serious consequences for the survivors. For example, the importance of chronic abuse and the role it plays in psychiatric illness have been virtually ignored. This chapter addresses this knowledge gap by summarizing the results of an investigation (with my sociologist colleagues Patricia Perri Rieker and Trudy Mills) into the relationship between physical and sexual abuse and psychiatric illness in a psychiatric inpatient population (Carmen et al. 1984; Mills et al. 1985). This is one of the few studies to compare the experiences of adult males and females in terms of both patterns of abuse and responses to the abuse.

Methods

To explore the relationship between violence and psychiatric disorder, the life experiences of patients were reconstructed through an in-depth examination of psychiatric inpatient records. The population for this retrospective study included all patients discharged over an 18-month period from an adult psychiatric inpatient unit at a university teaching hospital. The final sample consisted of 188 adult and adolescent male and female patients (123 females and 65 males) (Carmen et al. 1984).

A standardized coding instrument was used to content analyze the discharge summary and other patient records for the following: demographic information; social, medical, and psychiatric histories; behavior before and during hospitalization; and details on the nature of the violence. Violence was defined as any form of serious physical or sexual abuse described in the discharge summary or in the record. These abuse events included child abuse, incest, and marital violence, as well as physical and sexual violence occurring outside of the family.

Extent of Abuse

Patients who were physically or sexually abused or both represented 43 percent of the psychiatric inpatient population we studied. Abuse was suspected but not confirmed in enough detail in the records of an additional 7 percent. Of the 80 abused patients, 53 percent (42) had been physically abused, 19 percent (15) had been sexually abused, and 29 percent (23) had been physically and sexually abused. Forty-one percent of the abused patients had been abused by more than one person. Ninety percent (72) of the abused patients had been abused by family members. Two-thirds (25 of 38) of those who had been sexually abused had been abused by family members.

Female patients were much more likely than males to have histories of abuse. Fifty-three percent (65) of the females and 23 percent (15) of the males had been abused. There were also differences between sexes in the patterns of abuse. Males (mostly teenagers) were most frequently abused by parents during childhood and adolescence, whereas females were abused by parents, spouses, and strangers. For the females, abuse started in childhood and continued through adulthood. Only four of the 38 patients who had been sexually abused were males, as were their assailants. Seventy-five percent of the 28 teenagers had been abused, compared with 39 percent of the adults.

Comparison of Abused and Nonabused Patients

Can abused patients be differentiated from nonabused patients in a clinical setting? To answer this question, we made comparisons on the basis of social history data, behaviors at the time of admission, and behaviors during the hospitalization. Diagnosis did not differentiate between abused and nonabused patients. One significant family characteristic of the abused patients was the excessive use of alcohol by parents. Thirty percent of the abused patients had alcoholic fathers, compared with 13 percent of the nonabused patients.

In further comparison of social history characteristics of abused and nonabused patients, we found that abused patients were more likely than nonabused patients to have past histories of suicidal and assaultive behaviors and criminal justice system involvement. The wide range of behaviors and symptoms displayed at the time of admission did not differentiate abused from nonabused patients.

Two important differences emerged when we examined various behaviors during hospitalization. First, abused patients tended to remain in the hospital longer than the nonabused group. Twenty-six percent of the abused group were hospitalized longer than 90 days, compared with 9 percent of the nonabused. The mean hospital stay for nonabused patients was 43 days, and for abused patients it was 58 days. The mean length of stay for victims of sexual abuse was 67 days; victims of physical abuse, 53 days. Abused females had longer stays (60 days) than abused males (50 days) (Mills et al. 1985).

Second, abused and nonabused patients differed in how they dealt with anger–aggression during the hospitalization. This is especially pertinent to our study, since anger is an expected response to abusive events. We developed a measure of the coping behavior of the inpatients that focused on whether the anger was mainly directed inward or outward and whether behavioral control of aggressive impulses was maintained. According to our anger–aggression coping typology, 20 percent of abused patients compared with 10 percent of nonabused patients directed their aggression inward in an uncontrolled and actively self-destructive fashion. This finding shall be discussed further when the issue of gender is examined.

21

Comparison of Abused Males and Females

The majority of the 15 abused males were teenagers (60 percent), and the majority of the 65 abused females were adults (81 percent). There were other differences between male and female abused patients. First, they presented themselves differently at the time of admission. The behavior of the abused females resembled that of the other females at the time of hospitalization; that is, they were equally likely to be suicidal or depressed. Abused males, however, differed from the other males at the time of hospitalization. They were *less* likely to appear depressed, suicidal, or psychotic and were *more* likely than nonabused males to be aggressive or to have disordered conduct or psychosomatic symptoms.

Other differences between abused males and females emerged when behaviors before hospitalization were examined. The abused males were much more likely than the abused females (and other males) to have abused others. Sixty percent of the abused males had been violent toward others while only 17 percent of the abused females had been violent. Abused males were also more likely than abused females (and other males) to have had criminal justice system involvement.

Perhaps the most important characteristic that distinguished the behavior of the abused males and females was that the males became more aggressive whereas the females became more passive. In some ways, the sex-role stereotypes seemed to be exaggerated in this sample. This was evident in the way that abused males and females coped with anger. Thirty-three percent of the abused males coped with anger by directing it aggressively toward others, but only 14 percent of abused females did so. In contrast, 66 percent of abused females directed their anger inward, often in an actively suicidal and destructive manner, compared with only 20 percent of the abused males. Abused males, more than nonabused males, coped with anger by aggressively directing it toward others, while abused females were more likely than other females to turn their anger inward. Victims who turned their anger inward were also more likely to have longer hospital stays.

Psychiatry and the Victim-to-Patient Process

Our finding that almost half of the psychiatric inpatients in our sample had histories of physical and/or sexual abuse is not surprising, given the prevalence and acceptance of violence in the general population. As this study demonstrates, most of the abuse occurred in the context of family. People who are abused by family members are more likely to be abused more than once, or for longer periods of time, so that the abused patients were a population of chronically victimized people. Although there are important psychological issues specific to particular kinds of abuse, our observations indicate a common pattern of responses to chronic victimization. Despite dramatic gender differences in both patterns of abuse and behavioral responses to abuse, we concluded that males and females alike sustained severe psychological trauma as a consequence of the abuse. The most enduring psychological legacy of chronic abuse is a disordered and fragmented identity. This is observed clinically in the form of low self-esteem and self-hatred, affective instability, poor control of aggressive impulses, and disturbed relationships with inability to trust and to behave in self-protective ways (Rieker and Carmen 1986).

We know that not all victims become mental patients. How can we understand the processes that cause such enduring damage to self? *All* victims of physical and sexual abuse are faced with a complex series of social, emotional, and cognitive tasks in order to make sense of experiences that threaten body integrity and mortality. Confrontations with violence challenge one's most basic assumptions about the self as invulnerable and intrinsically worthy and about the world as orderly and just. After victimization, the victim's view of self and world can never be the same again. The working-through process involves a reconstruction of self and world that incorporates the abuse experience (Janoff-Bulman and Frieze 1983; Rieker and Carmen 1986).

The universality of the cognitive and affective processes set into motion by the abuse is well documented in the literature on psychic trauma and stress response syndromes. Such responses consist of involuntary recurrences of thoughts, feelings, and behavioral reenactments of the trauma alternating with periods of denial, psychic numbness, and behavioral constriction as a way of warding off the repetitive intrusions. At the heart of these processes is the necessity, at least temporarily, of dissociating or distancing oneself from affects and experiences that threaten to overwhelm an individual's adaptive capacities.

When the assailant is an intimate or a family member, these processes are further complicated by the profound betrayal of trust and the chronic vulnerability to physical and psychological danger when the abuser has continuing access to the victim. It was not uncommon, in our study population, for a patient to have experienced multiple kinds of abuse. We observed a pattern of increased vulnerability of female victims to other kinds of abuse; it is unclear if such vulnerability to multiple abuse is the same among males with prior histories of victimization (Carmen and Rieker 1984).

Victim responses are also shaped by the chaotic and destructive psychologic processes and relationship patterns that characterize many violent families (Rieker and Carmen 1986). For example, in abusive families, the child or adult victim's survival is often contingent on accommodating to a family system in which exploitation, invasiveness, and the betrayal of trust are normal and loyalty, secrecy, and self-sacrifice form the core of the family's value system. In a sense, the victim's survival is dependent on adjusting to a "psychotic" world where abusive behavior is acceptable but telling the truth about it is sinful. It is hard to convey the terror, helplessness, vulnerability, and loneliness of these victims. This isolation of victims is further reinforced by their helpless dependency and shame, offenders' threats of retaliatory violence, and the disbelieving responses of potential helpers outside the family (Rieker and Carmen 1986).

Clinicians generally ask patients about abuse experiences if they have some reason to suspect abuse. However, these suspicions are often based on unfounded stereotypes about victims and violent families. Increasing awareness of the extent of violence in our society might lead one to suspect that psychiatric patients are more likely to have experienced physical or sexual violence than to hear voices, yet clinicians are systematic in their inquiries about hallucinations while overlooking the reality and importance of violent assaults. Our research and that of others underscore the discrepancy between the alarming numbers of people who are physically and sexually abused and the lack of attention given these topics in psychiatric theories or therapies.

Despite the advances in knowledge about victimization, there remains great confusion in psychiatry about its relevance for understanding and treating mental illness. Many clinicians adopt theoretical perspectives that deemphasize the social realities that lead to psychological disorders, thus minimizing the connection between victimization and illness. The American Psychiatric Association's proposal to include masochistic personality disorder as a diagnosis in the *Diagnostic and Statistical Manual of Mental Disorders (Third Edition-Revised)* (American Psychiatric Association 1987) revision is one of the clearest examples of how a psychologic disorder can be viewed in isolation from one's life experiences. In this way, victims are blamed and labeled, rather than understood. The failure of child abuse experts to have noticed that mothers were being battered in these same families and the continuing failure of many clinicians to recognize that there are severe psychologic consequences of child abuse for the adult survivors are other examples. The failure of psychiatrists to notice or even wonder that half of psychiatric populations have abuse histories is consistent with these patterns of denial.

Unfortunately, when clinicians do not link these abuse experiences with their patients' psychologic disorders, victims are again left in isolation with their secrets and their pain. Contrast this denial with the national attention to the posttraumatic stress responses of Vietnam veterans who have received needed services and compensation for their war-related disorders. There are no memorials for the victims of family violence, who have been engaged in a domestic war as surely as our veterans were engaged in a foreign war (A National Agenda 1985).

It is crucial that clinicians begin to appreciate that victims of physical and sexual violence already constitute a sizable part of the population of the chronically mentally ill, and that the chronically mentally ill are at very high risk for additional victimization. Since most victims have not had the benefit of early intervention, mental health professionals must recognize the persisting effects of abuse as these are manifested in posttraumatic stress and other disorders in order to promote recovery.

Of equal importance is the establishment of a direction for a legislative agenda aimed at prevention. We need to identify the social policies that leave women and children vulnerable to physical and sexual abuse. Are there policies that can be developed to prevent these forms of violence? There need to be alternatives for women and children other than remaining in violent relationships. These alternatives must include easy access to contraception and abortion; the development and enforcement of uniform child support policies; high-quality day care; equal educational, vocational, and economic opportunities; and the availability of counseling and support services that are sensitive to the needs of victims.

References

American Psychiatric Association: Diagnostic and Statistical Manual of Mental Disorders (Third Edition-Revised).

Washington, DC, American Psychiatric Association, 1987

Carmen E(H), Rieker PP, Mills T: Victims of violence and psychiatric illness. Am J Psychiatry 141:378-383, 1984

Finkelhor D: Sexually Victimized Children. New York, Free Press, 1979

Hilberman E: Overview: the "wife-beater's wife" reconsidered. Am J Psychiatry 137:1336-1347, 1980

Janoff-Bulman R, Frieze IH (eds): Reactions to victimization. Journal of Social Issues 39(2):1983

Mills T, Rieker PP, Carmen E(H): Hospitalization experiences of victims of abuse. Victimology: An International Journal 9:436-449, 1985

A National Agenda to Address Women's Mental Health Needs: A Conference Report. A joint project of the American Psychological Association, Women and Health Roundtable, and Federation of Organizations for Professional Women, 1985

Rieker PP, Carmen E(H): The Gender Gap in Psychotherapy: Social Realities and Psychological Processes. New York, Plenum, 1984

Rieker PP, Carmen E(H): The victim-to-patient process: the disconfirmation and transformation of abuse. Am J Orthopsychiatry 56:360-370, 1986

Russell DEH: The prevalence and incidence of forcible rape and attempted rape of females. Victimology: An International Journal 7:81-93, 1982

Russell DEH: Sexual Exploitation: Rape, Child Sexual Abuse, and Workplace Harassment. Beverly Hills, CA, Sage, 1984

Stark E, Flitcraft AH: Spouse abuse. Surgeon General's Workshop on Violence and Public Health Source Book, October 1985

Recognition and Treatment of Incestuous Families

JUDITH HERMAN, M.D.

Chapter 3

Recognition and Treatment of Incestuous Families

*I*ncest, the sexual abuse of children within their families, is a major mental health problem that until recently has gone largely unrecognized within the mental health professions. Several large-scale surveys of predominantly white, middle-class populations have consistently documented the fact that about *10 percent of all women report a childhood sexual experience with an older male relative, and at least one percent of all women have had a sexual experience with a father or stepfather* (Kinsey et al. 1953; Landis 1956; Finkelhor 1979). The risk to boys is not as well documented, but some clinicians believe that cases involving male victims may be significantly underreported (Dixon et al. 1978). When boys are molested within their families, the abuser is as likely to be a father as a mother (Maisch 1972; Meiselman 1978; Justice and Justice 1979).

Incestuous abuse usually begins when the child is between the ages of 6 and 12, though cases involving younger children, including infants, have been reported. The sexual contact typically begins with fondling and gradually proceeds to masturbation and oral–genital contact. Vaginal intercourse is not usually attempted, at least until the child reaches puberty. Physical violence is not often employed, since the overwhelming authority of the parent is usually sufficient to gain the child's compliance. *The sexual contact becomes a*

Reprinted with permission from Herman J: Recognition and treatment of incestuous families. International Journal of Family Therapy 5:81–91, 1983.

compulsive behavior for the father, whose need to preserve sexual access to his daughter becomes the organizing principle of family life. The sexual contact is usually repeated in secrecy for years, ending only when the child finds the resources to escape. The child victim keeps the secret, fearing that if she tells she will not be believed, she will be punished, or she will destroy the family (Summit 1982).

Incestuously abused children exhibit a wide variety of distress symptoms including nightmares, bed-wetting, fearfulness, social withdrawal or misbehavior, and somatic complaints, particularly lower abdominal or pelvic pain (Brandt and Tisza 1977; Burgess and Holmstrom 1978a; Sgroi 1978). Symptoms in adolescence include runaway attempts, suicide attempts, drug and alcohol abuse, hysterical seizures, indiscriminate sexual activity, and early pregnancy (Herman 1981; Goodwin 1982). The destructive effects of the incest appear to persist into adult life, long after the sexual contact has ended. Adult women with a history of incest have persistent and often severe impairments in self-esteem, intimate relationships, and sexual functioning (Meiselman 1978; Herman 1981). Incest victims also apparently run a higher than normal risk for repeated victimization (battering and rape) (Herman 1981). Marriage to an abusive spouse, with potential repetition of the abuse in the next generation, is a frequent outcome (Goodwin 1982).

Recognizing the Incestuous Family

Incest occurs in all social classes and racial and ethnic groups. The vast majority of cases, probably over 90 percent, never come to the attention of any social agency (Gagnon 1965). Poor and disorganized families are heavily overrepresented among reported cases because they lack the resources to preserve secrecy.

Incestuous families are not easily recognizable because of their conventional appearance. In most cases, the family structure represents a pathological exaggeration of generally accepted patriarchal norms. Incestuous fathers are often well respected in their communities. They are frequently described as "good providers," and their wives are often completely dependent on them for economic survival. Incestuous fathers often attempt to isolate their families, restricting both the mobility and the social contacts of their wives and daughters. It is not unusual for the daughters to report that their mothers cannot drive a car, that the family never has visitors, or that they are not allowed to participate in normal peer activities because of their fathers' jealousy and suspiciousness. Finally, incestuous fathers often enforce their dominance in the family through violence. In a survey of 40 women with an incest history, over half reported having witnessed their fathers beating their mothers or other children (Herman 1981). The daughter singled out for the sexual relationship is usually spared the beatings; however, she understands clearly what might happen to her if she incurs her father's displeasure.

For these reasons, incestuous fathers are often described as "family tyrants" (Weinberg 1955; Cormier 1962; Maisch 1972). However, once the incest has been detected, they are unlikely to present in this manner in a clinical interview. On the contrary, they commonly appear as pathetic, meek, bewildered, and ingratiating (Walters 1975). Because they are exquisitely sensitive to the realities of power, they rarely attempt to intimidate anyone who has equal or greater social status, such as an adult professional. Rather, they will attempt to gain the professional's sympathy and seek to deny, minimize, or rationalize their abusive behavior. *Inexperienced professionals may incorrectly conclude that the father is a relatively powerless figure in the family and may even describe the family system as mother dominated.*

Most mothers in incestuous families, however, are not in any position to dominate their husbands; often they can barely take care of themselves and their children. One of the most consistent findings in the literature is the unusually high rate of serious illness or disability in mothers of sexually abused daughters (Maisch 1972; Browning and Boatman 1977; Finkelhor 1979; Herman 1981). Undiagnosed major mental illness—schizophrenia, depression, or alcoholism—is frequently observed in the mothers.

It should be noted also that one of the most common causes of maternal "disability" in the incestuous family is the mother's inability to take control of her reproductive life. Numerous surveys have documented the fact that incestuous families have more children than the prevailing norms (Tormes 1968; Lukianowicz 1972; Maisch 1972; Herman 1981).

Economically dependent, socially isolated, battered, ill, or encumbered with the care of many small children, mothers in incestuous families are generally not in a position to consider independent survival, and must therefore preserve their marriages at all costs, even if the cost includes the conscious or unconscious sacrifice of a daughter.

Incestuous fathers do not assume maternal caretaking functions when their wives are disabled; rather, they expect to continue to receive female nurturance. The oldest daughter is usually deputized to take a "little mother" role, often assuming major responsibility for housework and child care (Kaufman et al. 1954; Lustig et al. 1966; Justice 1979; Herman 1981). The daughter's sexual relationship with the father often evolves as an extension of her other duties. As the oldest daughter reaches adolescence and becomes more resistant, the father may turn his attention sequentially to the younger daughters. Repetition of the incest with more than one daughter or with other available children (nieces, stepchildren, grandchildren) has been a common finding of numerous reports (Cavallin 1966; Herman 1981).

Sexual estrangement of the marital couple is frequently cited as a factor in the genesis of incest. However, careful interviewing of offenders and their wives indicates that most incestuous fathers continue to have sex on demand with their wives as well as their daughters; those fathers who confine their sexual activities to their children do so by choice (Groth

1979). Similarly, alcoholism, though frequently observed in the fathers, does not seem to play a determining role in the development of overt incest; problem drinking is reported as frequently in fathers who are seductive but not overtly incestuous, and in the general population (Herman 1981). To be sure, many fathers attempt to excuse their behavior by attributing it to "demon alcohol"; however, careful interviewing again reveals that the compelling sexual fantasy is present when the father is sober. He may drink in order to provide a "time out" during which he can disclaim responsibility for his actions (Groth 1979).

To summarize the known risk factors: Father–daughter incest should be suspected in any family that includes a violent or domineering and suspicious father; a battered, chronically ill, or disabled mother; or a daughter who appears to have assumed major adult responsibilities. Though the oldest daughter is particularly vulnerable, once incest has been reported with one child, all other children to whom the father has intimate access should be considered at risk. Incest should also be suspected as a precipitant in the behavior of adolescent girls who present as runaways, delinquents, or with drug abuse or suicide attempts.

In situations where these risk factors are present, questions about incest should be incorporated into the initial interview. Indeed, given the known prevalence of incest, a case can be made for including questions about sexual contacts between adults and children routinely in all evaluations. The main obstacle to obtaining a history of incest is the clinician's reluctance to ask about it. Incest provokes strong emotional reactions even among seasoned professionals. Denial, avoidance, and distancing are universal responses. Clinicians may have particular difficulty considering the possibility of incest in families of similar racial, ethnic, religious, or class backgrounds to their own, while families that are comfortably different may be more easily suspected.

For a clinician who has mastered these countertransference reactions, obtaining a history does not present unusual difficulties. Calm, direct questioning is often sufficient. For children, some specialized interviewing techniques have been developed; these include the use of drawings and anatomically correct dolls (Burgess and Holmstrom 1978b; Goodwin 1982; Adams-Tucker 1982). Using these materials, even very young children are able to describe what has happened to them and to distinguish fantasy from reality. False complaints of sexual abuse are rare; on the other hand, it is common for a child to retract a true allegation under pressure from the family (Goodwin 1982).

Crisis Intervention

The discovery of incest represents a major family crisis, requiring rapid and decisive intervention. Usually, by the time of the disclosure, the incest has been going on for several years, and the family's defenses have been organized around preservation of the incest secret. Disclosure represents a serious disruption to established patterns of functioning and a threat to the survival of the family. The father faces loss of the sexual activity that has become an addiction. He also faces possible loss of his wife and family, social stigmatization, and even criminal sanctions, though in practice these are virtually never applied. The mother faces possible loss of her husband, social stigmatization, and the terrifying prospect of raising her family alone, a task for which the mother is usually ill prepared.

In this situation, the father usually reacts by maintaining steadfast denial. He insists that the child is lying and directs his efforts to persuading his wife and outsiders that he is innocent. The mother finds herself torn between her husband and her daughter. Though she may initially believe the child and attempt to take protective action, unless she receives rapid and effective support she will usually rally to her husband's side within a week or two. If she persists in believing her child, she has a great deal to lose and very little to gain. The daughter, therefore, may find herself discredited, shamed and punished for bringing trouble on the family, and still unprotected from continued sexual abuse. Suicide and runaway attempts are particularly likely at this time. Without effective intervention, the child may be scapegoated and driven out of the family.

Unfortunately, most therapists are not well prepared to intervene in this crisis, because they fail to recognize incest either as criminal or as addictive behavior. This can be seen most commonly in the resistance to the use of criminal terms, "offender" and "victim," and in the failure to report incest to child protective agencies, even though such reporting is mandated by law. Naive therapists may tend to accept the offender's denial or his assurances that the sexual abuse has stopped. Therapists may also be seduced by the offender's rationalizations, all of which are widely supported in popular and professional culture. The most common rationalizations are first that incest is harmless, or would be if not for prudish social condemnation; second that incest is consensual and children are willing participants; and third that incest is simply a response to deprivation of adult sexual expression and can be treated as such.

Failing to recognize the criminal and addictive nature of the abusive behavior, the therapist may approach the family as though incest were merely a symptom of family dysfunction. He may attempt to treat the underlying dynamics, using a traditional individual or family therapy model in which the therapy contract is freely chosen, one therapist assumes full treatment responsibility, and the rule of confidentiality is observed. This model, which is useful and appropriate for neurotic and some psychotic patients, is ineffective for addicts and for character-disordered patients who commit crimes. Successful crisis intervention with incestuous families requires an active, directive, even coercive approach, and it requires ongoing cooperation between the therapist and agencies of the state: law enforcement and child protective services. No therapist can treat incest alone (Summit 1981).

Because the problem of incest has only recently claimed the serious attention of mental health professionals, principles and techniques of therapeutic intervention are still in the early stages of development. Successful intervention with the incestuous family clearly requires a high degree of institutional coordination, clinical sophistication, and plain hard work. Well-documented treatment outcome studies do not as yet exist, and even published program descriptions are rare. The following treatment guidelines are derived from site visits to five of the most fully developed treatment programs in different areas of the country and from verbal reports of clinicians working in 40 to 50 other programs. They represent an attempt to define points of consensus and of controversy among experienced clinicians in the field. A fuller elaboration of these guidelines may be found elsewhere (Herman 1981).

The initial focus of crisis intervention should be on stopping the sexual abuse and establishing a safe environment in the family. Reporting to the mandated authorities should be done promptly, preferably in the presence of the family, and should be explained as a protective, nonpunitive measure. The therapist must assume that the child's complaint of sexual abuse is valid and should not be confused by initial denial on the part of the parents.

Once the incest has been reported, debate often revolves around whether or not the child should be temporarily removed from the home. In some cases this appears to be the only practical means of ensuring the child's safety. However, this intervention is destructive to the child for several reasons. First, it makes her feel that she has done something wrong and is being punished by banishment from her family; second, it reinforces the tendency of the parental couple to bond against the child; and third, it is difficult to find an appropriate placement for the child. If safety cannot be guaranteed at home, it is much preferable to have the father leave during the crisis period. Unfortunately, child protective agencies do not have the legal authority to remove a parent from the home; however, this result can often be accomplished either by persuasion or in some states through the use of civil protection laws. A court order may be obtained requiring the father to vacate the home and to provide child support for a limited time. Conditions for supervised visitation and for mandated treatment may also be established by the court. Clinicians working with incestuous families should become familiar with these legal procedures.

During the crisis period, all family members are in need of intensive support. The child needs to be assured that there are protective adults outside her family who believe her story and will not allow her to be further exploited. She should be praised for her courage in revealing the incest secret, assured that she is not to blame for the incest, and told that she is helping, not hurting, her family by seeking outside help. She should also be told explicitly that many children retract their initial complaints and that she will not be abandoned should this happen in her case. The mother needs help believing her daughter and resisting the tendency to bond with her husband against the child. If the couple separates, the mother also needs help with issues of practical survival. Previously untreated health problems should also receive prompt attention. The father needs help facing the fact that secrecy has been irrevocably broken and that he must now admit and give up the sexual relationship with his daughter before the family can be restored.

The crisis initiated by the revelation of the incest secret is resolved at the point at which the family is under the supervision of the mandated agency and a coordinated treatment plan is in place. Cooperation between all professionals working with the family facilitates quick and effective crisis intervention and greatly improves the prospects for treatment.

Treatment in the Postcrisis Period

Following the crisis of disclosure, the incestuous family is generally so divided and fragmented that family treatment is not the modality of choice. Experienced practitioners who have begun programs with a family therapy orientation have almost uniformly abandoned this modality except in late stages of treatment (Giarretto et al. 1978; Summit 1981). Group treatment for mothers, fathers, and child victims appears to be a far more promising approach. In some cases, individual, couple, or family therapy may be recommended in addition to group. For all family members, the issues of stigmatization, isolation, and poor self-esteem are especially amenable to group treatment. For fathers, group treatment is effective also in breaking through denial and rationalization of the criminal behavior. Many group programs for offenders follow a highly structured model similar to programs for the treatment of alcoholism and other addictions. In early stages of treatment, the offender acknowledges that he has lost control of his behavior and must submit to external control. Progression through the program involves increasing acceptance of responsibility for present behavior and restitution to others for past abuses (Silver 1976; Brecher 1978).

Opinion is divided on whether incest offenders can be motivated to remain in treatment without a credible threat of criminal sanctions for failure to comply. To date, the most highly developed treatment programs for incest have been those that rely on a court mandate (Giarretto et al. 1978; Berliner 1981). No program has yet demonstrated an ability to engage offenders in sustained treatment without legal sanctions.

In addition to group and individual treatment, many programs incorporate a partial self-help component, most frequently called Parents United and Daughters and Sons United. Self-help activities supplement more formal therapeutic work in a number of ways. During the crisis period, the family's intense need for support may be met by frequent peer contact. The father in particular may be more easily persuaded to admit the incest and cooperate with a treatment program if he is rapidly put in contact with other offenders who have successfully participated in treatment. In the postcrisis period, families beginning treatment may benefit from the experience of those further along, while "advanced" group members may gain self-esteem from being in a helping role. Finally, after formal treatment is terminated, self-help groups provide a continued source of support and community.

Criteria for Terminating Treatment

Restoration of the incestuous family centers on the mother–daughter relationship. On this point, there seems to be wide consensus among experienced practitioners, even those most committed to reuniting the parental couple (Giarretto et al. 1978). Safety for the child is not established simply by improving the sexual or marital relationship of the parents; it is established only when the mother feels strong enough to protect herself and her children, and when the daughter feels that she can turn to her mother for protection.

The father may be judged ready to return to his family when he has admitted and taken full responsibility for the incest, apologized to his daughters in the presence of all family members, and promised never to abuse his children again. When the father is ready to return to the family, the family may or may not be ready and willing to receive him. This choice properly rests with the mother, once the mother–daughter bond has been restored, and once neither mother nor daughter feels intimidated. A decision for divorce may be as valid as a decision to rebuild the marriage; certainly the preservation of the parents' marriage should not be considered the criterion of therapeutic success. Probably the best gauge of successful treatment is the child victim's subjective feeling of safety and well-being, the disappearance of her distress symptoms, and the resumption of her interrupted normal development.

Given the present state of therapeutic knowledge, no one can claim to "cure" incest; rather, the behavior may be brought under control, first by outside intervention, second

41

by empowering the mother as a protective agent within the family system, and finally, to a limited degree, by developing the father's inner controls. The father's internal controls should never be considered sufficient to ensure safety for the child; if the family decides to reunite, mother and daughter should be explicitly prepared for an attempt to resume the incestuous relationship (Groth 1979). Some degree of outside supervision should probably be maintained as long as children remain in the home.

Further investigation is needed in order to continue the development of effective treatment of all family members. Direct clinical studies of incestuous fathers are still quite rare and largely confined to convicted offenders, who comprise a very small and skewed sample. Long-term follow-up studies of treated and untreated families, and comparative studies of differing treatment approaches are needed in order to document what is at present part of the oral culture of recent clinical experience.

References

Adams-Tucker C: Early treatment of child incest victims. Paper presented at the Annual Meeting of the American Psychiatric Association, Toronto, 1982

Berliner L: King's County approach to sexual abuse, in Innovations in the prosecution of child sexual abuse cases. Edited by Bulkley J. Washington DC, American Bar Association, 1981

Brandt R, Tisza V: The sexually misused child. Am J Orthopsychiatry 47:80-90, 1977

Brecher E: Treatment programs for sex offenders. Washington DC, U.S. Government Printing Office, 1978

Browning D, Boatman B: Incest: children at risk. Am J Psychiatry 134: 69-72, 1977

Burgess A, Holmstrom L: Accessory-to-sex: pressure, sex and secrecy, in Sexual Assault of Children and Adolescents.

Edited by Burgess A, Gross A, Holmstrom L, Sgroi S. Lexington, MA, D.C. Heath, 1978a

Burgess A, Holmstrom L: Interviewing young victims, in Sexual Assault of Children and Adolescents. Edited by Burgess A, Gross A, Holmstrom L, Sgroi S. Lexington, MA, D.C. Heath, 1978b

Cavallin H: Incestuous fathers: a clinical report. Am J Psychiatry 122:1132-1138, 1966

Cormier B, Kennedy M, Sangowicz J: Psychodynamics of father–daughter incest. Canadian Psychiatric Association Journal 7:203-215, 1962

Dixon K, Arnold E, Calestro K: Father-son incest: underreported psychiatric problem? Am J Psychiatry 135:835-838, 1978

Finkelhor D: Sexually Victimized Children. New York, Free Press, 1979

Gagnon J: Female child victims of sex offenses. Social Problems 13:176-192, 1965

Giarretto H, Giarretto A, Sgroi S: Coordinated community treatment of incest, in Sexual Assault of Children and Adolescents. Edited by Burgess A, Gross A, Holmstrom L, Sgroi S. Lexington, MA, D.C. Heath, 1978

Goodwin J: Sexual Abuse: Incest Victims and Their Families. Boston, MA, John Wright, 1982

Groth N: Men Who Rape: The Psychology of the Offender. New York, Plenum Press, 1979

Herman J: Father–Daughter Incest. Cambridge MA, Harvard University Press, 1981

Justice B, Justice R: The Broken Taboo. New York, Human Sciences Press, 1979

Kaufman I, Peck A, Tagiuri C: The family constellation and overt incestuous relations between father and daughter. Am J Orthopsychiatry 24:266-279, 1954

Kinsey AC, Pomeroy WB, Martin CE et al.: Sexual Behavior in the Human Female. Philadelphia, PA, Saunders, 1953

Landis J: Experiences of 500 children with adult sexual deviation. Psychiatr Q (supp) 30:91-109, 1956

Lukianowicz N: Incest. Br J Psychiatry 120:301-313, 1972

Lustig N, Dresser J, Murray T, et al: Incest. Arch Gen Psychiatry 14:31-40, 1966

Maisch H: Incest. New York, Stein & Day, 1972

Meiselman K: Incest. San Francisco, Jossey-Bass, 1978

Sgroi S: Child sexual assault: some guidelines for intervention and assessment, in Sexual Assault of Children and Adolescents. Edited by Burgess A, Gross A, Holmstrom L, Sgroi S. Lexington, MA, D.C. Heath, 1978

Silver S: Outpatient treatment for sexual offenders. Social Work 3:134-140, 1976

Summit R: Beyond belief: the reluctant discovery of incest, in Women's Sexual Experience. Edited by Kirkpatrick M. New York, Plenum, 1982

Summit R: Sexual child abuse, the psychotherapist, and the team concept, in Dealing with Child Sexual Abuse. Chicago, National Committee for Prevention of Child Abuse, 1981

Tormes Y: Child Victims of Incest. Denver, CO, American Humane Association, 1968

Walters D: Physical and Sexual Abuse of Children. Bloomington, IN, Indiana University Press, 1975

Weinberg S: Incest Behavior. New York, Citadel, 1955

Chapter 4

Self-Help and Advocacy: An Alternative Approach to Helping Battered Women

DEBORAH WILLIAMS-WHITE

Chapter 4

Self-Help and Advocacy: An Alternative Approach to Helping Battered Women

It is by now commonly accepted that America is a violent society. But this acceptance does not automatically bring with it a realization that for the typical citizen, the problem is not violence in the streets, but violence in the home. (Roy 1977)

Intrafamily violence has become an all too familiar occurrence in American homes. Abuse of children, siblings, parents, and spouses is a violent crime being committed in homes that are perceived to be safe refuges. According to the Federal Bureau of Investigation's 1984 Uniform Crime Report, in 18 percent of that year's 18,692 murders, the victim was the wife. An acquaintance was the victim in 30 percent of the cases and a stranger in 18 percent (Federal Bureau of Investigation 1984). *Intrafamily violence is the most frequent crime committed, yet it is the most underreported crime in the United States.*

One of the most pervasive of family violence crimes is spouse abuse. This chapter focuses on spouse abuse and methods of intervention for its victims based on self-help and advocacy. Spouse abuse is a crime that, until recently, was not recognized as an important social problem, although

47

women have been the victims of domestic violence throughout history.

In the United States laws were established to provide guidelines for brutality against women based on the old English common-law doctrines. These laws explicitly permitted wife beating for the purpose of correcting behavior deemed inappropriate by husbands. One such law, known as the Rule of Thumb Law, permitted a husband to beat his wife with a stick no larger than the circumference of his thumb. It was the end of the 19th century before such laws were repealed. Yet, as late as the 1970s, an old town ordinance in Pennsylvania prohibited a husband from beating his wife after 10:00 P.M. or on Sundays. American courts did legally rule against a man's right to beat his wife; however, this did not assure the safety of women because hostility and aggression acted out by husbands against wives was viewed as a private matter. Furthermore, documentation of the crime was deliberately denied, and the victims were encouraged for the sake of family solidarity to keep silent. A national crime survey from the year's 1978 through 1982 found that an estimated 2.1 million married, divorced, or separated women were victims at least once in 12 months of rape, robbery, aggravated or simple assault by their partners. Within an average of six months, 32 percent of these women were victimized again by their partners (Innes and Langan 1980). According to a national crime survey for the years 1973 through 1981, men commit 95 percent of all assaults on spouses (Federal Bureau of Investigation 1982).

The structural, cultural, and social characteristics of our society continue to perpetuate the victimization of women on all levels. Women are the constant victims of male dominance, and they are perceived to be the property of their husbands or partners to do with as the latter choose. The fight for equality in the workplace has not automatically assured equality in the home.

Largely because of the efforts of the battered women's movement, shelters for victims, support groups, and community awareness programs have been established to provide assistance to victims of domestic violence.[1] Providing shelter for battered women and their children and helping victims discover ways to lead violence-free lives are major focuses of the battered women's movement. Many women who were once silent have now found that they do have an opportunity to speak out and receive help. Because the mere existence of shelters and their advocates cannot end domestic violence, many battered women turn to human service workers, mental health professionals, police, and judicial officers for assistance. Therefore, careful examination must be given to the services we currently offer the battered woman and to the impact of these services for stopping violence against her. How we respond may well determine whether a woman breaks the cycle of violence she is in or continues to be victimized.

Self-help and advocacy programs have proven to be viable alternatives to traditional practice methods when working with battered women. Self-help and advocacy are skills that can be effectively used outside of the shelter environment and incorporated into all programs that provide services to women who are battered. Consequently, it is imperative that we begin to explore the positive role self-help, advocates, and advocacy programs can play in eliminating violence against women.

Victims

Battered women represent all age, racial, religious, cultural, educational, and socioeconomic groups. Battered women are housewives and executives, married and single. An abused woman is subjected to repeated physical and/or mental battering by someone who may profess to love her. The abuse

---

[1] For the purpose of this chapter, the term *battered women* refers to both married and unmarried women since women who are not legally married are also victims of domestic violence. In addition, the terms *spouse abuse* and *domestic violence* will be used interchangeably.

is rarely limited to an isolated episode, but instead usually increases in severity and frequency. More than one million women seek medical care for injuries caused by battering each year. Twenty percent of emergency medical services to women are caused by battering (Slitcraft and Stark 1984). A battered woman lives with the constant threat of being attacked. Often, despite repeated abuse, she cannot anticipate when the battering will occur.

Lenore Walker, psychologist, author, and noted expert on battering, states that battered women commonly have low self-esteem, adhere to feminine sex-role stereotypes, and inappropriately accept the responsibility themselves for the batterer's actions. Abused women suffer from guilt, anger, fear, shame, and isolation from friends, family, and support systems. The individual battered woman may even have doubts about her sanity. The battered woman's feelings of helplessness consequently cause her to relinquish control of many other aspects of her life. Over time she may begin to have difficulty making and carrying out decisions concerning the options available to her. This further intensifies her feelings of helplessness and reinforces her inability to act on her own behalf; this behavior is often referred to as "learned helplessness."

Commonly, a battered woman may feel she must stay in an abusive relationship for the sake of her children. Initially, she may recognize and/or have few or no resources of her own. Battered women are often legitimately afraid of being followed, harassed, and possibly subjected to more serious violence if they should leave or take other actions against their abusers.

The mixed signals of love and hate that battered women receive from their batterers continue to reinforce their sense of hopelessness and confusion. A relationship marked by violence, yet at the same time interspersed with kindness and affection, makes it all but impossible for the battered woman to take decisive action. Unquestionably, victims of domestic violence must be helped to validate their sense of self-esteem and self-worth so that they feel able and competent to make decisions about their lives and carry their decisions through to action.

Responses to Victims

Already stated elsewhere in this volume, but important enough to bear repetition, is the fact that helping professionals must begin to acknowledge violence against women as representative of a larger social problem, rather than continue to treat women in a clinical or therapeutic fashion that in itself implies that the victim must have a psychologic disorder. Because battered women do turn to psychotherapists, including psychiatrists, psychologists, and social workers, these professionals must begin to focus on the effects of battering and not on the psychologic profiles of the victims. Stopping the battering is the most important concern for battered women and should be as important to all professionals in any treatment plan they devise. Instead of trying to restructure the personality of the battered women, helping professionals need to move toward helping battered women avoid victimization.

The common therapeutic model of treatment may also force the battered women to accept responsibility for the violence, intensifying their notion that they are at fault while reinforcing society's attitude of blaming the victim. In addition, this model of treatment continues to place the victim in an unequal position of power concerning her own needs. A woman who is seeking any type of assistance must be allowed to evaluate what form of assistance she desires.

The most effective assistance to battered women can be achieved by the helping professional's 1) acknowledging the existence of abuse; 2) taking steps to encourage the victim to stop the battering by removing herself from the abusive site, then helping her to strengthen her coping abilities and sense of power; and 3) helping her to clarify the mixed emotions she experiences.

Self-help, as it is defined when working with battered women, enables a victim to confirm her own capabilities, strengths, and power. It is important for her to recognize that each decision she makes adds to her personal growth. "Self-help, closely related to definitions of 'empowerment,' described as a process through which women, experts about their own lives, learn to know their strengths" (Schecter 1982, p. 109). As battered women develop their strengths, they begin to increase their self-esteem, confidence, and sense of independence. Self-help can also occur through the coming together of victims of domestic violence and the building of support networks. Through this bonding process, based on shared and common experiences, women can move forward to a new awareness of their collective strength and power.

The *self-help model* for working with battered women assumes that

1. Every woman has the capacity to use resources to meet her needs; some women are more proficient than others in doing so.
2. Each individual woman is the authority about her needs and what will work best for her.

Self-help may be the catalyst for the battered woman to make change. The process of empowerment through self-help can begin with the acknowledgment that it is she who initiated some change in the abusive relationship. Continued achievements enable the victim to realize that she need not depend on the batterer or on others to control her life. As formerly battered women increase their self-esteem by continuing to accept responsibility for themselves, they are in better positions to protect their own interests and to determine their future goals.

Advocacy is a means of providing practical and emotional support to battered women and is fundamental to the self-help process. Advocates of the antibattering movement work in support of and in conjunction with women who seek to live in a violence-free environment. Whether in a one-on-one counseling support system or in other areas, the advocate supports the abused woman's interests and goals, to create an awareness about and to work toward the eradication of domestic violence. The counseling advocate is instrumental in letting the battered woman know that her feelings are valued and that her opinions and ideas are credible. In order to be effective, anyone working as an advocate for battered women must believe that the battered victim can make healthy decisions and do what is in her own best interest. Furthermore, the advocate must display a high level of trust and acceptance. As an advocate, it is important to keep in mind that battered women need emotional as well as practical support if they are to expand their internal resources and coping abilities as well as their knowledge of services available to them.

The *Advocacy Skills Manual of the Pennsylvania Coalition Against Domestic Violence* emphasizes five major areas of concern for advocates working with battered women:

1. Support
2. Self-awareness education
3. Information and instruction
4. Accompaniment
5. Intervention

Since not all victims will need assistance in every area of concern, when helping victims evaluate their needs each task should be considered distinct from the others.

One of the most important skills to use as an advocate is the *ability to be supportive.* We can help to reassure women who are battering victims that their feelings are legitimate, and at the same time help them to put their feelings into reasonable perspective. Support can be offered through our patience, understanding, and encouragement.

Self-awareness education is practiced as we assist the victim on the road to rediscovering her ability to identify her specific strengths and weaknesses. Only by understanding both will she be able to view herself realistically.

Information and instruction are important to the discovery of resources and services that may be available to the victim. The advocate must know the scope of services available and how to use them.

Some advocacy responsibilities will include *accompanying the victim to services*, either simply to provide her support or because the advocate's assistance is actually needed to obtain the information or service needed. Often when a resource is not adequately serving the victim, the advocate may be requested to intervene on the victim's behalf. Intervention does not always mean handling the problem. Often it means assisting the victim to handle the problem herself.

Just as we must not assume that all battered women are in need of therapeutic treatment, we should not assume that all battered women will have the same concerns in advocacy. It is important to establish what goals the client has and which focus will best help her to achieve her goals.

At My Sister's Place, a Washington, D.C. shelter, the first step in working within the guidelines of self-help and advocacy begins with the victim's call to the hotline. Victims are offered emotional support, referrals, and an opportunity to express their feelings. It is emphasized that the woman has made an important step on her own behalf by reaching out for help. Whether the caller is interested in coming to the shelter or in choosing some other option, the hotline listener, who has been trained in advocacy and self-help skills, encourages the caller to determine what action she will take, based on what the caller feels is most appropriate for her. The listener may give different options and the possible consequences of those actions, but it is the woman who decides how she will proceed. Callers who do not feel ready to leave the abusive relationship are offered a Safe Plan. This Safe

Plan is designed to help women living with abusive partners to avoid injury and to help begin the practice of self-help. These callers are encouraged to formulate plans of where they will go should they be attacked. They are encouraged to decide what important papers they should have copies of should they not be able to return home. They are also encouraged to think about the importance of keeping money put aside and even obtaining a spare set of car keys. Finally, callers are encouraged to seek help at support groups and through family and friends.

One out of eight callers finds a safe refuge in the residential center. The residents are offered individual and group counseling. While in the shelter, each resident is in control of her own plans and desires. With the guidance and assistance of the advocates, a victim is helped to sort out her immediate and long-term needs. Women work on such concerns as legal matters, housing, employment, education, child care, and emotional stability. Each victim determines what plan of action best suits her and, with the advocate, how best to reach her goals. Advocates work not as directors, but as guides, sounding boards, and support systems. The concept of self-help is impressed upon each resident. Each woman is responsible for participating in shared household duties, support groups, and the general concern of the shelter. The time spent at My Sister's Place can be a time of personal growth, self-evaluation, and achievement.

Advocacy skills should not be limited to women's shelters. Instead, they should be available in hospitals, private physicians' offices, social service agencies, and the legal and educational systems, as well as in shelters. Some advocates will need to make use of all five areas of concern while others will focus only on specific areas.

1. *Hospital personnel and private physicians* must be willing to
   a. recognize that injuries reported by women may have occurred as the result of beatings;

    b. talk with the victims and convey a willingness to discuss abuse as a crime;

    c. assure victims that they are not at fault;

    d. encourage women to contact services available for battered women;

    e. make complete documentation on official records of all incidents; and

    f. consider strongly whether prescription drugs such as tranquilizers should be given to battered women.

2. *Mental health professionals* must be willing to

    a. acknowledge domestic violence as a major social problem;

    b. place victims in equal positions of power in determining goals;

    c. provide practical and emotional support;

    d. assure victims that they are not at fault; and

    e. consider alternative methods of intervention, based on self-help skills.

3. *Police officers and members of the criminal justice systems* must be willing to

    a. talk with the victim alone and convey willingness to discuss abuse as a crime;

    b. acknowledge domestic violence as a crime;

    c. convey that the victim is not held responsible;

    d. encourage the victim to seek help at a shelter or other appropriate victim assistance agency;

    e. keep the victim safe while she removes personal effects from the violent home such as clothing, eyeglasses, medication;

    f. document events in official records;

    g. inform the abuser that a crime has been committed and that the victim has legal recourse; and

    h. provide the victim with the officer's name, badge number, report number, and follow-up telephone number.

4. *Social service workers* must be willing to

    a. consider the need for services based on the victim's

    current economic status;
  b. place victims of domestic violence on priority listings for public housing; and
  c. provide access to a wide range of services.
5. *Educators* must be willing to
  a. develop curricula centered around dispelling sex-role stereotypes;
  b. develop curricula that encourage the growth of self-esteem and self-worth; and
  c. develop a model for responding to children believed to be from violent homes.

Conclusion

Individuals and programs working with battered women must take a comprehensive approach to providing services to victims. We cannot adequately work on the issues of low self-esteem, guilt, anger, and isolation until we acknowledge that many of these behaviors are the result of continued involvement in violent relationships. The battering of a woman should not be regarded as an isolated incident, but rather as a problem that will affect a woman's entire existence.

The experience of shelter workers and counselors has shown that self-help and advocacy programs are effective tools for assisting victims of domestic violence crimes. Over time these methods must become more widely used and accepted by mental health and human service professionals. These methods are not intended to replace the traditional clinical therapy that has been used to assist abused women. However, professionals should not assume that the only successful method that helps abused women is traditional clinical therapy. To do so may very well perpetuate the victims' learned helplessness as well as continue to reinforce women's feelings that they are to blame for being battered. Rather, for some victims of domestic abuse it may be a combination of clinical treatment and self-help that is of most personal and lasting benefit. Finally, it is imperative that the therapist/worker examine the needs of each battered victim as an individual and work in conjunction with the victim to establish plans and goals leading to a violence-free life.

References

Barnett ER, Landis L: Handbook for Abused Women. National Clearing House on Domestic Violence, 1981 (Domestic Violence Monograph Series No. 8)

Chapman R, Gates M: The Victimization of Women (Volume 3, Sage Yearbooks in Women's Policy Studies). Beverly Hills, CA, Sage Publications, 1978

Combs AW: Helping Relationships—Basic Concepts for the Helping Profession. Boston, Allyn & Bacon, 1985

Dobash RE: Violence Against Wives: A Case Against Patriarchy. New York, New York Press, 1979

Federal Bureau of Investigation: Crime in the United States. Uniform Crime Report. Washington, DC, Federal Bureau of Investigation, 1982

Federal Bureau of Investigation: Crime in the United States. Uniform Crime Report. Washington, DC, Federal Bureau of Investigation, 1984

Hart WL, Ashcroft J, Burgess A: Attorney General's Task Force on Family Violence—Final Report, 1984

Innes LA, Langan P: Special Report: Preventing Domestic Violence Against Women. Washington, DC, Bureau of Justice Statistics, 1986

Janosik EH: Crisis Counseling, A Contemporary Approach. Wadsworth Health Sciences Division, 1984

Loving N: Responding to Spouse Abuse and Wife Beating, A Guide for Police. Washington, DC, Police Executive Research Forum, 1980

Martin D: Battered Wives. San Francisco, Glide Publications, 1977

Massachusetts Coalition of Battered Women Services Groups: For Shelter and Beyond: An Educational Manual for

Working with Women Who Are Battered. Massachusetts Coalition of Battered Women Services Groups, 1981

My Sister's Place, A Washington D.C. Shelter for Battered Women and Their Children: Volunteer Training Manual and Resource Guide. Washington, DC, My Sister's Place, 1985

NiCarthy G: Getting Free, A Handbook for Women in Abusive Relationships. Seattle, WA, Seal Press, 1982

Quiring LMT: Advocacy Skills Manual. Pennsylvania Coalition Against Domestic Violence, 1979

Roy M (ed): Battered Women: A Psychological Study of Domestic Violence. New York, Van Nostrand Reinhold, 1977

Schecter S: Women and Male Violence: The Visions and Struggles of the Battered Women's Movement. Boston, South End Press, 1982

Slitcraft A, Stark E: Medical Therapy as Repression: The Case of the Battered Woman. Wife Abuse: The Facts. Washington, DC, Center for Women's Policies, 1984

Walker LE: The Battered Woman. New York, Harper and Row, 1979

CAMROSE LUTHERAN COLLEGE
LIBRARY

Stages of Anti-Sexist Awareness and Change for Men Who Batter

DAVID ADAMS, M.Ed., C.A.G.S., L.C.S.W.

Stages of Anti-Sexist Awareness and Change for Men Who Batter

Wife Abuse: A Brief Social Overview

The battering of women by their husbands or boyfriends is a widespread social problem in the United States. Although estimates of its frequency among married couples vary widely (from 4 to 60 percent), even the most conservative of these estimates means that 1.8 million women annually are beaten by their husbands (Straus et al. 1980). Annual police and FBI statistics reveal that domestic disturbances are the most frequent problems for which police are called (Langley and Levey 1977). The majority of these domestic disturbances are reported to be cases of wife abuse. Schechter (1982), in her excellent history of the battered women's movement, reports that since the first emergency shelter for battered women opened in 1973, 400 others have been established across the nation. Nearly all of these shelters and safe home networks were founded and operated by women themselves. Leghorn (1977) observed that this system of women's shelters constitutes a vast network of underground railways for women and their children attempting to escape physical abuse from their husbands. Clearly, we live in a violent culture, and

This article is based on a paper presented at the Ninety-Second Annual Convention of the American Psychological Association, Toronto, August 24, 1985. I acknowledge and appreciate the assistance, suggestions, and other editorial help provided by the other members of the Emerge collective.

when one considers that rape and wife abuse are the most commonly reported violent crimes in America (Brownmiller 1975), it becomes evident that the victims of much of this violence are women. Ironically, despite public clamor about violence on the streets, statistically a woman is much more likely to be raped or beaten by her husband in her own home than by a stranger on the streets (Brownmiller 1975).

The alarming regularity of violence against women has propelled feminists to see rape and battering not as isolated incidents or acts of individual pathology but as symptoms of a sexist society (Martin 1981; Leghorn 1977; Warrior 1978). Many believe that these problems will not go away until their sexist underpinnings have been exposed and eradicated (Schechter 1982). For this reason, shelters for battered women and rape crisis centers have made it a priority to provide anti-sexist education, not only to women but to the community at large. Of particular concern to women's advocates have been those institutions such as the police, the courts, hospitals, and counseling agencies that most directly respond to what has traditionally been categorized as "domestic disturbances." As Schechter (1982) notes, it has only been because of the persistent community educating efforts of the battered women's movement of the past ten years that public awareness about rape and battering has grown and the traditional response of blaming the victim has begun to be reversed.

This chapter focuses on the need for programs that work with male batterers to adopt an anti-sexist perspective and approach. In the first section, I briefly review more traditional clinical approaches before building the case for a pro-feminist approach that integrates psychological work with anti-sexist education. The last section presents the findings of a small-scale research project that shows the sexist attitudes and defensive patterns of abusive men at three stages of treatment at Emerge, a pro-feminist batterers' program in Boston.

Traditional Treatment Approaches for Abusive Men

How one treats the abusive man depends a great deal on how one understands the problem. Those who see battering as a symptom of a dysfunctional marital system, for instance, are likely to offer conjoint or family therapy. Those who see battering as indicating individual pathology, on the other hand, are likely to provide long-term individual treatment or some form of inpatient care.

From a psychodynamic perspective, battering behavior is attributed to such underlying problems as impulsivity, poor frustration tolerance, low self-esteem, feelings of inadequacy, fear of intimacy, counterdependency, or developmental delays due to deficient parenting. Myers (1983), for example, believes that abusive men suffer from chronic fears of abandonment and often feel "narcissistic injury" when their partners fail to take care of them in expected ways. He therefore argues for an "invitational, nonthreatening" therapeutic approach that provides opportunities for men to express these feelings and to learn to better care for themselves. Other psychodynamic approaches seek to help violent men gain insight into the familial roots of their feelings of inadequacy and dependency (Garnet and Moss 1982; Gilligan 1981).

Less insight-oriented approaches see violence as resulting from skills deficits, such as difficulty dealing with stress or with communicating expectations in a direct manner (Neidig 1984; Novaco 1978). Sonkin and Durphy (1982) use assertion training and other social skills teaching techniques to help battering men become more adept at expressing feelings and resolving conflict in a nonaggressive manner. "Anger control training" and "anger management" have become some of the most widely recommended strategies for counseling batterers (Goffman 1984; Deschner 1984; Margolin 1979). The objective is to help men learn to recognize the cognitive, somatic, and situational cues to their potentially explosive anger so they can redirect it or take the time to express it in more appropriate ways (Ganley 1981).

Despite these differences in causal explanation for violence, psychodynamic and cognitive–behavioral approaches have something in common. They both see battering as essentially an exaggerated response to internal or external stress. In psychodynamic terms, the batterer overcompensates because of particular intrapsychic or character problems, while cognitive behaviorists would say that his responses are exaggerated because he hasn't acquired the skills or cognitive inclination to respond in more appropriate ways.

In this author's clinical experience, all of these psychological explanations are partially correct, but they cannot sufficiently account for the fact that so many men beat their wives (Roy 1977). To focus exclusively on anger, impulsivity, low self-esteem, skills deficits, or any other intrapsychic factor as the sole cause of violence is misleading and dangerous. Many men experience feelings of inadequacy and insecurity, for instance, yet they do not beat their wives. Many nonabusive individuals who lack basic social and coping skills do not beat their wives. On the other hand, many men who do beat their wives also demonstrate that they possess appropriate social and interpersonal skills in their interactions with co-workers and others. Why then are some men violent toward their wives and others not?

Looking at what men get out of violence may assist in adequately understanding its cause; that is, its *functional utility* may tell us more about why it occurs on such a large scale than its *psychologic etiology* can on the individual level. Violence is quite simply a controlling act. When a man is violent toward his wife, he often gets what he wants—whether that be his dinner, preventing her from going out, or the last word in an argument. Another instrumental effect of violence is that it tends to create fear, doubts about self-worth, and dependency in the victim, particularly when it is accompanied by routine psychological abuse.

A Vignette

My experience in my own family of origin helps to illustrate this point. My father's regular physical and verbal abuse of my mother caused her to develop grave doubts about herself and her ability to make it on her own. After several years of their marriage, she began to internalize my father's criticisms of her and to doubt her own perceptions about his shortcomings. Because my father also isolated my mother from her friends and relatives, she had little outside validation or support from which to challenge his ill-treatment of her. She became dependent on him for approval that he rarely gave. When approval is kept scarce, it is rendered more valuable. Thus, my father's withholding of approval and affection became just as controlling as his physical violence.

A Pro-Feminist Treatment Approach

That male violence serves as an instrument of male control is the feminist analysis of battering. Moreover, as the above example illustrates, violence is but one aspect of male control, though one that makes more covert controls such as yelling, criticism, accusations, and the withholding of approval more effective. The existence of male violence within intimate relationships and within our culture means that male anger and male disapproval have come to serve as subliminal reminders of male violence, according to Dworkin (1983). Brownmiller (1975) has observed that rapists are the shock-troopers of a male-dominant society. Because some men rape, all women must limit their mobility, watch what they wear, and generally restrict their actions vis-à-vis men. Likewise, because some men batter, all women must be wary of male anger and fearful of confronting male authority. Many professional women I know have told me they feel they need to be very cautious about questioning what their male colleagues "know." These women say that they are fearful of arousing male anger or righteous indignation so they usually keep their opinions to themselves or find indirect ways of getting their ideas across.

Besides physical and psychologic controls, sexism consists of institutional controls that permit men to define men's experience of reality as right and proper for all, says Wilson-Schaef (1981). This means that since men dominate such knowledge-encoding and culture-seeking institutions as history, psychology, medicine, religion, art, and the news media, male standards and perspectives constantly color our understanding of reality. As Adrienne Rich has observed, "Objectivity, as we know it, is nothing more than male subjectivity made unquestionable" (1979). On the level of interpersonal politics, men often dismiss women's arguments on the grounds of their being "illogical" or "overly subjective." Since male biases and standards are institutionalized, all men can claim a certain entitlement to "the truth" as they see it. Wilson-Schaef (1981) believes that this ability for men to define reality is the essence of sexism. She compares sexism and male standards to smog, in that it pollutes the air in ways that we don't see once we have become habituated to living in it. Eitzen (1982) states that sexism, like racism, has three different but interlocking dimensions: violence, discrimination, and prejudice. Every form of oppression needs a supportive ideology. Once a class of people is devaluated, it is easier to justify abusing and discriminating against them.

A Vignette

An Emerge client expressed a commonly held attitude among abusive men when he commented to his fellow group members, "It didn't seem like any big deal, abusing my wife; she wasn't going anywhere. I guess I just never took her that seriously; I kinda took her for granted."

Sexism is defined here as a system of interconnected male controls consisting of physical and psychological controls, derogatory beliefs about women, institutional (reality-defining) controls, and policies that discriminate against women. The presence of this social system of male controls reveals the inadequacy of exclusively psychologic interpretations of battering behavior. Violent men do not exist in a vacuum. Wittingly or unwittingly, their behavior reinforces (and is reinforced by) patriarchal social norms and plays an integral part in the overall system of male dominance. Therefore, explanations for male violence toward women must include the political as well as the psychologic dimensions of the problem. The political dimensions of battering mean its controlling effects as well as the social and personal ideologies that support it. In terms of the individual batterer, this perspective means looking at what he gets out of being violent and how he justifies his violence. Adams and McCormick (1982) state that in order for a man to be violent, his belief system must include 1) a belief in violence as a legitimate way of solving problems and 2) a belief that it is okay for men to control women.

In order for any treatment program for abusive men to be successful, it must tackle both these sets of beliefs. However, these attitudes are not as easily detectable in the abusive man as one might believe. When asked, for instance, if they think violence is an acceptable way of solving problems or if it is legitimate for men to control women, many batterers say "no." In other words, there is a contradiction between these men's professed beliefs and their behavior. This type of contradiction indicates the inadequacy of evaluating or determining people's true attitudes according to self-assessment. Feminist researchers like Dobash and Dobash (1979) have questioned the ability of men, as reflected by their behavior, to accurately assess their own attitudes toward women. For example, Leghorn and Warrior (1979) cite surveys that show that though many men believe they devote an equal amount of time as their wives to housework and child care, closer examination of the fact reveals otherwise. Certainly, Phillips and Derman-Sparks (1982) support the idea that behavior is the best reflection of attitudes.

A second point to be stressed about sexist attitudes and attitude change is that anti-sexist education necessarily promotes changes in self-awareness as well as in social awareness. In their college courses on anti-racism, Phillips and Derman-Sparks (1982) find that as students become more aware of the social and institutional magnitude of racism, a period of personal crisis is provoked in which the students struggle to confront their own personal participation and complicity in racism. A new awareness emerges, previously denied, of racist attitudes and behaviors. For these students, as for others, denial is perhaps the major impediment to personal and social change.

With men who batter their wives, denial, together with minimization of both their violence and sexist control patterns, is probably the major reason why the overwhelming majority never seek help. This denial and minimization of battering on the individual level are reinforced by the denial and "conspiracy of silence" about it on the societal level. Of those abusive men who do seek therapy, many are court-mandated clients. While the Emerge program is not a court-mandated program, most of the clients seek help only after their partners have left home for an emergency shelter or obtained a Restraining and Vacate Order from the court that bans the husband from the home for a certain time period. In essence, these men are motivated primarily by their desire to get their wives back—rather than by a desire to change their violent behavior (Adams 1982). In fact, many terminate therapy once their partner has returned or the court order has lapsed. For nearly all of these men, their violence continues (Adams and Penn 1979; Rimm 1977).

The Emerge program consists of eight weeks of individual counseling and assessment followed by 6 to 10 months of group counseling and education. In contrast to many other treatment programs, a major emphasis is placed on anti-sexist education. One technique that is used by several pro-feminist programs to help men become more aware of their control patterns is assigning them to keep "control logs." Emerge instructs men to monitor themselves with the use of a written checklist of violent and controlling behaviors. Education is also provided about the damaging and controlling effects of each of the behaviors on the checklist. The Domestic Abuse Intervention Program in Duluth, Minnesota, uses videotaped portrayals of various violent and abusive behaviors in order to further sensitize men to their control patterns. Such exercises not only promote more accountability for men's behavior, but also create a keener awareness of the contradictions between the men's stated intentions (for example, "I just wanted to get her to listen to me") and the actual consequences (frightening her, pushing her away) of their actions.

Once the batterer has demonstrated a willingness to abstain from violent and controlling behaviors, more attention is directed to the attitudes, expectations, and feelings that have accompanied such behavior. The men's attitudes and expectations toward their wives usually indicate an *intent to devalue* rather than to understand their wives. This is evident in the ways that men report interactions with their partners. Rather than reporting what his wife actually said or did, the abusive man will usually *characterize* her words and actions in a mocking, trivializing, or otherwise denigrating manner. Comments like "She went on and on about nothing"; "She was in a bitchy mood"; and "There was no pleasing her" are examples of these characterizations. Even when pressed by group counselors to relate the specific content of the interaction, men cannot recall their wives' actual words or specific complaints, again indicating an intent to devalue and dismiss the concerns rather than an intent to understand them. Recognizing its importance to batterers, pro-feminist counselors take an active role in interrupting the devaluation process as it occurs within the counseling group. Men's devaluing comments about their partners and their selective accounts of marital interactions are questioned. Alternative and more validating ways of interpreting their partners' words and actions are elicited. At the same time, the contradiction is highlighted between the men's desire for their wives to feel closer to them and their continuing attempts to dismiss or trivialize their wives' concerns. The men are asked, "How *can* she feel closer or want to remain with you so long as you want to criticize and control her?"

On the basis of our clinical experience at Emerge, my colleagues and I believe that lasting abstinence from violence is possible only when men make attitudinal as well as behavioral changes. The importance of behavioral changes, however, cannot be discounted. Emerge clients are accordingly expected to make "safety plans" that will minimize the possibility for continued violence. Safety plans include respecting the woman's fears and stated limits about the relationship, fully complying with court protective orders, eliminating drug or alcohol use if it has accompanied violent behavior, and ceasing any pressure or intimidation tactics intended to change her plans or to deny her contact with others. Separate contact with the battered woman is also made (by the local battered woman's program or by Emerge) to apprise her of her legal protection options as well as of support, advocacy, and emergency shelter services. She is also validated in her perception of not being responsible for her husband's violence. She is clearly encouraged to ensure her own safety from continued violence as much as possible.

Contact with the partners helps Emerge counselors establish concrete and relevant treatment plans for each man. For instance, marital separation, with minimal contact between spouses, is often necessary so the man can work on his goals without continuing to pressure his wife or to demand continuous emotional caretaking from her at a time when she is struggling to establish her safety and independence from him. Once a man has made such a separation plan with the group (spelling out what his contact with his wife should be) his membership in the group becomes contingent on his living up to the plan. Thereafter, if he continues to harass or to put pressure on her to make a decision about the marriage, he is expelled from the group with a negative evaluation.

After the initial stages of group work in which the group counselors actively model supportive confrontation, listening, and a caring concern for others, the group members are usually able to take a more active role in challenging and supporting each other toward change. In effect, the group becomes an alternative male peer culture in which men can learn to express themselves more openly and to examine their own control patterns toward women and their children. They are also encouraged to relate less competitively and more openly with other men. Violent men tend to have few close friendships with other men or women, and this lack of other outlets for intimacy leads them to place unrealistic and often impossible expectations and demands on their wives to be their sole emotional caretaker (Adams and McCormick 1982). The partners of these men report that they feel a tremendous burden is placed on them to be responsible for the men's every and often unexpressed need.

The Study to Measure Changes in Attitudes and Controlling Behaviors

An attitudes survey was given to individual and group clients in order to test out some of my clinical impressions of developmental stages that men go through in confronting their violence and sexism. These 12 client surveys were followed by partner contacts in order to determine the level of the men's violence and control patterns. My first hypothesis was that men progress through three different phases of coming to terms with their sexist behavior and attitudes. A second hypothesis was that men in each stage have different levels of awareness of sexism and their own participation in it that accompany behavioral and self-identity changes. A third hypothesis was to see whether these attitudinal changes loosely correspond with some of the more socially integrative frameworks of adult psychological development such as those advanced by Kegan (1982) and Gilligan (1982); in other words, are there consistent psychologic correlates to given levels of anti-sexist awareness? In order to limit the scope of this survey, questions were included pertaining to just a few dimensions of attitude and identity change. The survey questions were

1. How would you briefly describe yourself as a person?
2. What does it mean to be responsible?
3. How would you describe your wife (or partner)?
4. What do you think causes (or caused) you to be violent toward your partner?
5. Can your partner make you angry?
6. Do you think that sexism is a problem in this country?
7. Do you participate in sexism in any ways? If yes, please give examples.
8. Have you made any changes as a result of the women's movement?

The first three questions were intended to gain a sense of how the abusive man sees himself, defines responsibility, and sees his partner when he is at a given stage of treatment and growth. Questions 4 and 5 were meant to show differences in how men attribute responsibility for their violence and anger. The last three questions were included to determine differences in how aware the men were of their own and societal sexism, and how much influence they attribute to the women's movement.

Twelve men were surveyed, and seven of these were videotaped during their interviews. Of the total men interviewed, two had received fewer than two sessions of counseling, eight were in the middle stages of treatment (5 to 20 sessions), and two had completed the full 32-week counseling program with a positive evaluation from partners and counselors. Thus, these men represented three different stages of treatment. The two men who had just entered the counseling program were still actively violent and controlling, according to the assessments of their partners and counselors. The eight men in the middle stages of treatment varied in the degree to which they had reduced their level of violence and other controlling behaviors. Five of these had not been violent since entering the program but were also still separated from their partners.

All but one of these men's partners reported that their husbands were still putting pressure on them (in the form of pleas, occasional outbursts of anger, and frequent phone calls or overstayed visits) to take them back, though all five partners also reported that they felt their partners had made significant progress in reducing controlling behaviors. Of the three middle-stage men who had reconciled with their partners, two had been violent once and the other had not been violent since beginning therapy. These men's partners also reported significant progress in reduction of controlling behaviors and other goals, but said that they still felt their husbands were controlling and critical at times. Both of the men who had completed the Emerge program had not been violent in the time since termination (six months for one and two years for the other), and each man's partner said that she was very pleased with her husband's progress and what she saw as his continuing efforts to grow. These partner assessments were given after the men were interviewed. All of the men interviewed are married and nine have children. One is black, one is Portuguese, one is Japanese-American, two are Jewish, and the remaining seven are of mixed European heritage. Their ages ranged from 24 to 45 and were fairly well distributed among the three groups.

Stages of Growth for Abusive Men

The survey results tended to support my clinical impressions of three different stages of growth in men's awareness of sexist attitudes and controlling behaviors. Despite differences in growth rate, the three groups showed surprising consistency in how each group differently framed and answered the same questions. Group differences were most evident in the responses to Questions 4 and 6 through 8, though notable differences were also apparent in Questions 1 through 3. The types of responses to Question 5 were more overlapping, but this may reflect the ambiguity of the question.

Survey results are integrated into the following description of the three stages of growth in anti-sexist awareness. The successive stages—denial, disequilibrium, and decision—best describe the level of awareness of individuals in each stage. There names are borrowed from the excellent work of Phillips and Derman-Sparks (1982) on anti-racist awareness education. Table 1 lists the common features of each stage.

Stage 1: Denial

Abusive men at the denial stage employ various defense mechanisms to avoid taking responsibility for their violence (Adams and Penn 1979), including minimization ("it was only a push" or "she bruises easily"), intentionality (claiming good intent, such as "I just want to get her to listen to me"), and the use of alcohol as an excuse. Other defenses include claiming loss of control ("something inside me snapped") and projecting blame onto one's partner ("she drove me to it" or "she started it with words"). These men are highly defensive and controlling toward their partners, respond to anger or accusations by making counteraccusations and becoming violent, and tend to be nonintrospective or introspective in rather selective ways. The man tends to deny his dependency on his partner for emotional caretaking while maintaining illusions about his own autonomy. He manages his self-esteem at his partner's expense by criticizing her, trivializing her concerns, and limiting her access to others. He is jealous and possessive, often accusing his wife of infidelity, and tends to be inflexible and dualistic in his thinking and in his response to conflict.

This type of man sees things in black-or-white terms and expects his partner and children to accept his interpretation of what is right. Said one man at this beginning stage, "I don't decide what's right or wrong; it's just common sense. She [his partner] should know that!"

TABLE 1. Stages of Growth for Men Who Batter

Stage	Predominant Coping Strategy and Features	Attitudes Toward Personal and Societal Sexism
1: Denial	Denial of problems ("I'm not violent")	Belief in male superiority (conservative) or equality of oppression (liberal)
	Projecting blame onto partner	Denial of personal and institutional sexism
	Claiming loss of control	Justification of sex roles or passive participation in sex roles
	Using alcohol as an excuse	"We're all in the same boat" mentality
	Minimizing of violence	Male-defined reality assumptions
	Citing good intentions	Women are dependent, weak, provocative and/or
	Violent and controlling behaviors	
	Physical violence	False idealization of women
	Frequent use of anger and criticism	Expectations of women as emotional caretakers
	Possessiveness and restrictiveness	Intolerance of women's anger
	Emotional withholding	Projected responsibility for feelings
	Unacknowledged dependency on partner	Sees partner as an extension of himself
	Manages self-esteem at her expense	Defines her according to role functions or in superficial ways
	Has illusions about his autonomy	
	Defensiveness (won't accept feedback)	Sees women as sex objects
	Contradictions between goals and actions	Relationships with men
	Inflexible and dualistic thinking	Superficial and limited
	Hostility toward partner	Engaged in male bonding at the expense of women
	Fears of abandonment	
	Internally generated stress	Resentment toward other women "for putting ideas in her head"
	Crisis (created by the wife's leaving or obtaining a court order)	Hostility toward women, particularly feminists
	Anger and bargaining	Anger toward partner "for making me look bad"
	Accusations of abandonment	
	Gift and flower giving	

TABLE 1. Stages of Growth for Men Who Batter *(continued)*

Stage	Predominant Coping Strategy and Features	Attitudes Toward Personal and Societal Sexism
	Promises to change	Sees her as crazy and unpredictable
	Escalation of violence	
2: Disequilibrium	Anger and bargaining	Defensiveness about sexism
	Blaming and accusations	Denial of impact on others
	Provisional commitment to counseling	Continued blame for feminists
	Cosmetic changes	Belief that "women have all the power"
	Shaky introspection	Expectation that partner will reward him for initial changes
	Some admission of problems and violence	Demands for attention and sex
	Recognition that he cannot always control partner	Grudging recognition that some women can make it on their own
	New distinctions made between his perceptions and reality	Mixed with anger and feelings of betrayal
	New awareness of feelings	Begins to see the world in less black-and-white, male-centered ways
	Guilt for past actions	Gains a greater recognition of the caretaking roles that women play
	Looking for a "quick fix"	Begins to gain perspective on his sexist expectations of women
	Confusion and despair	Begins to identify control patterns
	Questions past illusions about autonomy	Not listening; interrupting
	Identifies needs of others	Criticism or invalidation
	Fears loss of identity	Still depends on others to point these behaviors out but is less defensive
	Feelings of hopelessness	More understanding of women's reality
	More commitment to introspection	
	Identifies and begins to express feelings of hurt, fear, sadness, loneliness, and vulnerability	
	Shows greater tolerance for ambivalence	

	(previously defined as weakness or indecisiveness)	Differences are no longer seen as wrong or crazy
	Greater acceptance of responsibility for behavior	More acceptance of his partner's limits and boundaries
	More relatedness to others	Women's values and characteristics are more respected
	Greater empathy for other people's problems and feelings	
	More willingness to take risks with self-disclosure	
	Learns to negotiate conflicts rather than attempting to overpower or intimidate the other	
3: Decision	Commitment to personal change	Sees that the way things are defined is relative (according to the eye of the beholder) and accepts women's perspective as equally valid, and is able to learn from it
	More able to look at himself	Can accept women's anger without being defensive or making counteraccusations.
	Fuller ownership of feelings and behavior	Recognizes his own sexism as something he needs to continually examine and work on
	More able to initiate process reviews	Can talk openly about his sexism Challenges other men about sexism and supports them to change
	Recognition of interreliance and mutuality	
	Able to give to others without expectation of immediate gratification or return	
	Able to create his own support system	
	Can tolerate and respond to distress in others (not under- or overreacting)	
	Commitment to social responsibility and action	
	Feels need to share what he's learned with others	
	Engages in new activities and projects that use his new understanding of the world and his place in it	

It is important to stress that abusive men do not necessarily come across to those outside the family as controlling and inflexible. In fact, they often project an image to others as friendly, warm, outgoing, and helpful. Many of my clients at Emerge have been respected and admired in their communities and workplaces. Their inflexibility and controlling behavior tend to be restricted to their partners and (but not always) to their children. This type of split between public and private behavior makes it difficult for some people to believe that certain men they know could be wife abusers. In terms of overall psychological functioning, some of these men might be rated quite high on developmental scales that place an emphasis on individuality and autonomy because they are counterdependent, and the emotional caretaking they surreptitiously receive from their partners enables them to maintain a relatively high degree of personal functioning and competence with others. Similarly, some abusive men might be placed quite high on Kohlberg's scale of moral development, as their public expressions in appreciation for individual rights resembles what Kohlberg (1973) describes as Stage 4 morality.

The two survey subjects who were in Stage 1 counseling gave rather one-dimensional descriptions of themselves and their partners (Questions 1 and 3) in contrast to the men in the middle and later stages of therapy. Their self-descriptions tended to be overinflated and devoid of any references to their relationships to others, except in rather superficial or cliched ways.

Question 1. How would you briefly describe yourself as a person?

Ron: Personality-wise, very easy-going. I was in the service for seven years. I've been halfway around the world; the other half I'm not interested in. Adventurous. I'm willing to take chances to do things.

This kind of self-assessment fits Gilligan's (1982) analysis of men at a preaffiliative state. These men tend to describe themselves in terms of their achievements and separation from others, rather than in terms of their connectedness to others.

Responsibility was similarly defined in impersonal and cliched terms by both of these men. John defined it as "doing one's duty," while Ron talked of "the buck stops here." These men's descriptions of their wives were also quite superficial, with an emphasis placed on their wives' role performance rather than on personal characteristics.

Question 2. How would you describe your wife?

John: She's attractive. A good mother. She's good at saving money. We get along pretty good most of the time. That's all I can think of right now.

The abusive man at the denial stage does not really see his partner as a separate and viable other but rather as an extension of himself. His violence and criticism serve as messages to her to not be different.

In terms of awareness of sexism, there are two subtypes of abusive men in the denial stage. The more conservative, traditional man denies that sexism is a problem or an issue of consequence. He upholds the "natural" superiority of men over women and accepts the normative roles and prevailing division of labor between men and women as good for all. Sometimes, women are placed on a pedestal and overidealized in superficial and insipid ways. Ron's responses to Questions 6 through 8 typify this outright denial of sexism as a personal or societal problem:

Question 6. Do you think that sexism is a problem in this country?

Ron: Sexism? No, not really.

Question 7. Do you participate in sexism in any ways?

Ron: No.

Question 8. Would you say that you've made any changes as a result of the women's movement?

Ron: No.

By contrast, the liberal or nontraditional subtype of abuser tends to admit the existence of sexism, but also concludes that "men and women are in the same boat." This qualification means that because men are oppressed too, there are no significant differences between men's and women's positions in society. This liberal attitude is reflected by John's responses to Questions 6 and 7:

Question 6. Do you think that sexism is a problem in this country.

John: Yes. I don't believe that there are equal rights for the sexes in this country. I think it's better than it's been. I think it will probably continue to get better, but not at a sufficiently rapid rate to suit me. I also feel that there is some reverse discrimination—I'm thinking now of inequality of women to men. I think there is a smaller degree of reverse sexism in certain areas where a man is not treated equally, i.e., in terms of the man being a single parent and getting, you know, an equal opportunity to get custody of his children or even joint custody. I don't feel that male nurses are equally accepted throughout the profession where the nursing profession is dominantly female. I believe that the instances of reverse discrimination are fewer compared to sexism as we are basically discussing it. Nevertheless, I think it is there.

Question 7. Do you participate in sexism in any ways?

John: Absolutely not. Absolutely not. I am committed, committed against that. (He discusses at length that although he voted for Ronald Reagan, he was constantly at odds with Reagan's stand against the Equal Rights Amendment and against abortion.) I just don't approve of sexism in any way and I will not be party to it.

Though they differed on how much they saw sexism as a social problem, neither was willing to admit to personal sexism and both were also reluctant to attribute any influence to the women's movement in terms of their own attitudes. John characterized its influence as "negligible"—since he saw himself as already having nonsexist beliefs!

In summary, abusive men in the denial stage either deny the existence of personal problems or find ways to rationalize their actions. Their expectations and interactions with their partners indicate a lower level of functioning than is evident in the public sphere, where they seem more able to make distinctions between their own perceptions and reality. At home, however, there is what Kegan (1982) describes as an embeddedness in his own impulses, needs, and perceptions and a failure to tolerate his partner as a separate and viable other person. Moreover, there is an unacknowledged dependency on women for emotional caretaking and a general denial of sexism on the personal level as well as a minimization of it on the societal level. Unfortunately, most violent men at this stage never progress to Stage 2.

Stage 2: Disequilibrium

In order to reach disequilibrium, abusive men usually have to undergo a crisis. The crisis typically begins when the man's partner leaves him. Whether he progresses to Stage 3 or remains in Stage 1 depends on how much he can tolerate the initial confusion and terror that marks the boundary between Stages 1 and 2. This confusion and desperation comes from having one's assumptions and security challenged. Initially, all of the man's energy is mobilized into coercing his wife back. Walker (1979) calls this period of remorse following an incident of violence the "hearts and flowers stage" and says it often plays a maintenance role in perpetuating the "cycle of violence." (It should be noted, however, that not all men who batter experience remorse because of their actions.) After the separation, the man may variously resort to gift giving and pressure tactics, including violence, in his attempts to win the woman back. When she doesn't respond to these efforts, he may promise to seek counseling. Unfortunately, many abusive men enter counseling wanting guarantees of marital reconciliation and promptly drop out when guarantees are not given. This type of angry and manipulative behavior constitutes initial grief reaction to a loss that isn't yet accepted. This initial denial is accompanied by anger and accusations directed at the wife for abandoning and "humiliating" the man, and bargaining for her return with promises of changes and/or counseling. If these ploys don't work, the man becomes depressed and feels unable to care for himself. In therapy, he is very dependent on the therapist for a "quick fix" or formula for creating the appearance of change.

In my clinical experience an abusive man generally needs to progress through all five of Kubler-Ross's (1975) stages of grief before he becomes genuinely self-motivated to change; he must accept that he has no control over his wife's behavior before he can begin to examine his own behavior. In this disequilibrium stage, the abusive man's introspection is at first shaky and provisional, but there is a dawning recognition of the need to take responsibility for one's own behavior and feelings. In terms of self-development, he begins to relativize his feelings and perceptions and to place them within a broader context of other peoples' feelings and experience (Kegan 1982). The man grudgingly begins to recognize that his partner can exist apart from him, admits to a new acceptance of her autonomy, and comes to have a more multidimensional and ambivalent picture of his partner.

Question 3. How would you describe your partner?

Jack: Well, I haven't seen her for a while to talk to her. Joan, she's got a lot of problems but she works hard at taking care of our daughter, taking care of herself, and making a career for herself. Sometimes I think she's a little too selfish. But basically she's a really nice person. She has a lot of feelings. She cares for people, generally. She really works hard at being herself.

Ralph: I think the first word that would come to mind would be introverted. She's quiet. She's beautiful. She's very quiet. She's very thoughtful. She's always thinking about the next answer, you know, she always seems to be one step ahead.

These men's self-descriptions are also more ambivalent and self-reflective—indicating a greater introspection and tolerance of feelings and self-doubts that were previously suppressed.

Question 1. How would you briefly describe yourself as a person?

Walt: At this point, at the present moment? Lonely, but working hard at making myself a better person, getting in touch with my feelings. I have a lot of insecurities, but I'm really just trying very hard to make myself a better person, and fulfill a good life.

Walt's description of himself reveals a somewhat greater recognition of the connection between his feelings about himself and his relatedness and attachment to others. His definition of responsibility elaborates on this theme.

Question 3. What does it mean to be responsible?

Walt: Mostly, I've learned a lot about responsibility. It's really important to be responsible to myself, to go through every day being, you know, not making a fool of myself, hurting other people's feelings, trying to understand my own feelings, just trying to be a normal person.

Men in the disequilibrium stage of awareness are more able to express feelings of hurt, fear, loneliness, inadequacy, and dependency. This is significant in terms of their now being able to take responsibility for previously disavowed feelings that were often projected onto their partners, whom they saw as weak and "overly emotional." With the loss of control over others, there also comes a sense of loss of identity. This results in confusion and feelings of hopelessness and despair. Fogarty's (1979) compelling analysis of these feelings (which he generically labels as "emptiness") is quite pertinent to abusive men. Fogarty says that it is only when one accepts these feelings and stops running away from them that one can learn to grow. I find that male clients often attempt to conquer feelings of incompetence and insecurity, rather than accepting them as valuable parts of themselves that can lead to greater self-awareness and understanding of others.

At this stage, the abusive man's awareness of societal and personal sexism becomes more defined as his entire past vision of the world is called into question. Al's and Walt's responses to Questions 6 and 7 are typical.

Question 6. Do you think sexism is a problem in this country?

Al: Yes, I do. Just the way that women are treated every day. The way that men perceive women and their roles. I think also on the job they're not treated equally. I think they're exploited for their bodies a lot more than men would be. I think that's a problem.

Walt: Sexism? Yeah, it's definitely a problem. I don't think people understand what it's all about. I'm just beginning to understand it. At work, I notice how the men don't really listen to women when they're talking. Corporation presidents are mostly males, airline pilots, things like that; even the President doesn't seem to have a very positive attitude towards women.

Question 7. Do you participate in sexism in any ways?

Al: I think so, but I try to be conscious of it when I do it. I used to be a lot more sexist than I am now. I guess it's something I still need to think about, like being a better listener; that's one thing I need to work at.

Walt: Not so much now, but I probably did. Just the values that I have just being a man. I just had a man's point of view and looked at a woman as maybe a sex object. I just looked at her differently. I don't participate in it now, but I'm trying to understand it.

There is considerably more ownership of the problem as well as more congruence between the men's awareness of sexism on the societal level and their understanding of their own participation in it, though clearly there is still considerable resistance to seeing one's own sexism. There is also more willingness to recognize the influence and impact of the women's movement.

Question 8. Have you made any changes as a result of the women's movement?

Jed: Yes, I have participated more with my partner in conversation, work interests, education, etc. I'm much more assertive with people, have relaxed my dress and behavior. Generally I have become less of a playboy and have put less importance on being attractive to women. I have tried to show my feelings more even if they're not good ones.

In summary, though there are considerable shifts in attitudes and in responsibility for feelings and behavior at this stage, changes are still largely provisional and dependent on others (mainly counselors and partners) to make them worthwhile. Often, there is an expectation of rewards for every step along the way. While the man is looking for confirmation from his partner for his changes, she is often beginning to get in touch with her anger and independence and is less inclined to reward him for his new insights, many of which she had pointed out years earlier.

In lieu of confirmation from their partners, clients at this stage can become quite demanding toward their counselors because of the men's confusion and depression. In one sense, the counselors become the surrogate wives who are expected to become the emotional providers. Particularly at the beginning of the disequilibrium stage, the maturity and insights that the men exhibit in the group tend to evaporate once the men are in different settings. This means that they have not yet learned how to develop their own emotional supports or to monitor themselves on their own sexist attitudes and behaviors. Control patterns become more subtle, and for some men, more resistant to change; movement can be backward or forward. My clinical experience is that few men who batter progress beyond this stage despite months of counseling.

Stage 3: Decision

If the abusive man successfully negotiates his middle-stage confusion, depression, and dependency, he is able to gain a new perspective on himself and others that extends beyond the counseling group and his relationship with his partner. At the decision stage, the individual decides to become self-motivated to continue what he now sees as a lifelong process of self-evaluation and growth. Most important, he now becomes able to take more responsibility for his feelings, needs, and behavior. This means identifying his ongoing need for support and challenge from others. He begins to see himself as an autonomous individual with an interreliance on others for reciprocal support, recognition, and love. He is able to give to others without the expectation of immediate returns. He is capable of having both good and bad feelings about himself simultaneously, without the need to banish either set of feelings. This is manifested in Peter's self-assessment:

Question 1. How would you briefly describe yourself as a person?

Peter: Briefly, comfortably, I would describe myself as being depressed, searching, soul-searching, looking at a lot of issues about turning thirty, being successful, about . . . encouraged, I'm encouraged. I would also describe myself as—I'm losing the word for it right now—I'm feeling, I feel positive; I feel that very soon I will break through some stuff which has been making me feel unhappy.

Here, Peter seems able to accept his present feelings and yet place them in the perspective of recognizing that they will not necessarily persist or immobilize him. The partners of both of these men noted that their husbands are much more in touch with their own feelings and much more open to feedback from others than previously. These men are now able to fully recognize their partners as different and viable others (one of the men, Joseph, had been divorced by his wife, though they maintained friendly relations).

Question 3. How would you describe your partner?

Joseph: (laughing) My former partner, you mean. I'd say Janice is a very strong person. She gets depressed sometimes and gets down on herself but she's gained quite a lot of self-assurance since our divorce. She seems to have a very clear sense of herself and other people. She's got a good sense of humor, which I never noticed before, and she's modest, maybe overly so. Of course, we don't have as much contact with each other now so I don't know if she's changed in other ways or how she is to others. I think I can recognize her good qualities that I just couldn't see before.

Joseph shows full recognition of Janice as a separate individual, he recognizes the relativity of his own perspective on her and can also take into account her own self-perception and that she can be seen differently by others yet still be her own person.

Responsibility at the decision stage is seen as a combination of responsiveness to self and to others—much like Gilligan (1982) finds for women.

Question 2. What does it mean to be responsible?

Peter: To me, being responsible means looking at the impact I've had on other people. I've just recently described it as climbing over a wall of my own self-existence and looking up and seeing how I'm affecting other people. Owning things. Being able to give up the power associated with what's male.

Related to this, responsibility is now taken for one's own feelings as opposed to the tendency for men in previous stages of the process to make their partners responsible for the men's feelings.

Question 5. Can your wife make you angry?

Peter: (laughs) Can my wife make me angry? It seems like she has sometimes. No, I don't think she can make me anything. I recognize that I have a clear choice. That what I am, I have chosen to be. I immediately feel the effect of it but I am clear that I make my choices about how to react and how to be, how to think, how to behave.

Awareness of one's own sexism has sharpened to include more subtle control patterns such as interrupting women, emotional withholding, and passive compliance with sex roles. Moreover, the man no longer waits for others to point these dynamics out and is more capable of monitoring himself. There is a more complete congruence between one's awareness of sexism on the societal and the personal levels, and a genuine concern about its negative impact on oneself and others.

Question 6. Would you say that sexism is a problem in this country?

Peter: I would. I mean I see it as very oppressive and it's almost painful now for me to recognize it because I need to be responsible for it also. I see it everywhere. It's just been so costly when I think of more than half the people in the world, half the people in this country have just been cut off and stopped, squashed. I think of the physical realities of it. Women either being beaten or killed and being afraid to be out in the world, you know. When I think, when my wife mentions to me how she notices that when she walks down the street, she doesn't look at people's eyes because she can't do that without that being taken as an invitation for someone to invade her world.

Question 7. Do you participate in sexism in any ways?

Peter: How do I do that? There's many ways. I really interrupt a lot. How I control what we will talk about—this is not just with me and Carol, this is everywhere. I really, I really control the topic. I'll change a topic when I feel like changing the topic without noticing that I'm doing it that often. I notice that I'm wary of a woman, when I hear a woman make a statement about something, I might question it much more quickly than I would had a male made the same statement. Another thing I do is: "Well, they don't *really* know what it's like"—you know, women don't really know what it's like so that statement's kind of naive, or it's innocent and when they find out what it's really like, then I can say, "Didn't you know? Didn't you know that it's really like this?"

What is evident here—in contrast to John's response of Stage 1 and Al's of Stage 2—is a real openness to concede and confront one's own sexism. It bears mentioning that the level of sexism that Peter describes in himself is not unusual for men in general. What's unusual about it is his willingness to talk about it in a self-critical way. There is also for men at this stage an increased recognition of the impact of the women's movement, and a willingness to give credit to women for their greater consciousness about issues of sexism and control.

Question 8. Have you made any changes as the result of the women's movement?

Joseph: I would say it's really opened my eyes to a lot of things I was blind to before. I'm much more able to look at myself and sometimes I don't like what I see. In the past, I'd feel extremely threatened if something was pointed out to me, by a woman I mean. I mean, I think I would see her lips moving but I really didn't hear what she was saying if you know what I mean. I'm a better listener now—but I still love to talk (laughs). I'm spending more time with my daughter; that's different. I used to do more things with my son. When I hear a sexist joke about a woman, I'll speak up about it. I'll say, "Hey, wait a minute . . ." Before I'd probably just laugh or not say anything.

A final dimension of growth for this decision stage manifested by Peter and Joseph is the commitment to social responsibility and action; the decision to share what one has learned with others. In other words, the man begins to take battering and other forms of sexism on as a personal cause. The extent of this social commitment varies from man to man, but generally there is a new acceptance of personal and social responsibility that involves different interactions with others. For some men, this entails challenging sexist behavior when they see it in other men. For others, it means getting involved in feminist or men's group projects. Peter, for instance, has become an active volunteer counselor and public speaker at Emerge. Joseph has decided to coach a Little League team and says he wants to work with the boys on being less competitive and more cooperative with one another.

Conclusions

Psychological explanations can be seductive. Though they give us much helpful insight into individual and intrapsychic dynamics and motivations behind problem behavior, they do not by themselves adequately explain why social problems like wife abuse exist. Psychologic explanations can lead us away from placing the individual with his attitudes, feelings, and behaviors within a social and political context of patriarchally derived norms. Unfortunately, exclusively psychologic approaches have sometimes unwittingly perpetuated male violence by focusing only on the woman or by not confronting the real issue of man's violence as an instrument of control. For example, to focus exclusively on violence as a problem of anger management and communication is to only help the violent man become a more subtle and successful manipulator of women. Sadly, many therapists have been overaccommodating to angry and manipulative men and therefore have unwittingly protected their clients from the natural consequences of their own actions. When the abusive man is confused, he is not in control. At this point, the therapist must use this opening to encourage the man to engage in critical self-evaluation and movement forward. The therapist's hesitancy to talk about or confront the violence and the accompanying control patterns will be mirrored by the client's. The therapist should also not protect the abusive man from his confusion by supplying all the answers or by pressuring his partner to participate in therapy with him in order to create an unsound alliance with him that is unsafe for her as well as untherapeutic for him (Geller 1982). The abusive man must be held accountable for his controlling behaviors and attitudes toward women.

Therapists must also constantly bear in mind that counseling is not the only solution. Battering is a crime and therapists need to regard it as such. Any approach that focuses exclusively on individual and psychologic change, as opposed to institutional and political change, is doomed to failure, since sexist attitudes and behaviors on the individual level are socially sanctioned and reproduced. It is essential to make these connections between the psychologic and political and to understand the ways that political structures and hierarchies shape individual feelings, attitudes, and behaviors. The work to eradicate male violence toward women demands both social and individual change, confrontation and compassion.

References

Adams D: A group model for violent husbands. Paper presented at the American Orthopsychiatric Association's annual meeting, Boston, April 1982

Adams D, McCormick A: Men unlearning violence: group work with men who batter, in The Abusive Partner: An Analysis of Domestic Battering. Edited by Roy M. New York, Van Nostrand Reinhold, 1982

Adams D, Penn I: Groups for men: the socialization and resocialization of men who batter. Paper presented at the American Orthopsychiatric Association's annual meeting, New York, April 1979

Brownmiller S: Against Our Will: Men, Women and Rape. New York, Simon & Schuster, 1975

Deschner J: The Hitting Habit: Anger Control for Battering Couples. New York, Free Press, 1984

Dobash R, Dobash R: Violence Against Wives: A Case Against The Patriarchy. New York, Free Press, 1979

Dworkin A: Right-Wing Women. New York, Perigee Books, 1983

Eitzen S: In Conflict and Order: Understanding Society (Second Edition). Boston, Allyn & Bacon, 1982

Fogarty T: On emptiness and closeness, in The Best of the Family: 1973-1978. Edited by Pendergast E. Washington, DC, Georgetown University Family Center, 1979

Ganley A: Court-Mandated Counseling for Men Who Batter: A Three-Day Workshop for Mental Health Professionals (manual). Washington, DC, Center for Women's Policy Studies, 1981

Garnet S, Moss D: How to set up a counseling program for self-referred batterers: the AWAIC model, in The Abusive Partner: An Analysis of Domestic Battering. Edited by Roy M. New York, Van Nostrand Reinhold, 1982

Geller J: Conjoint therapy: staff training and treatment of the abuser and the abused, in The Abusive Partner: An Analysis of Domestic Battering. Edited by Roy M. New York, Van Nostrand Reinhold, 1982

Gilligan C: In a Different Voice. Cambridge, MA, Harvard University Press, 1982

Gilligan J: Individual, familial and social causes of violence. Paper presented at the Violence in the Family Conference, sponsored by the Laboure Center, Boston, January 1981

Goffman J: Batterers Anonymous: Self-Help Counseling for Men Who Batter Women. San Bernardino, CA, B.A. Press, 1984

Kegan R: The Evolving Self. Cambridge, MA, Harvard University Press, 1982

Kohlberg L: Collected Papers on Moral Development and Moral Education. Cambridge, MA, Moral Education Research Foundation, Harvard University, 1973.

Kubler-Ross E: Death: The Final Stage of Growth. New York, Prentice Hall, 1975

Langley R, Levy R: Wifebeating: The Silent Crisis. New York, E.P. Dutton, 1977

Leghorn L: Social responses to battered women. Speech delivered to the Wisconsin Conference on Battered Women, Madison, March 1977

Leghorn L, Warrior B: The Houseworker's Handbook. Cambridge, MA, Women's Center, 1979

Margolin G: Conjoint marital therapy to enhance anger management and reduce spouse abuse. Am J Fam Therapy 7:2, 1979

Martin D: Battered Wives (revised edition). San Francisco, Glide Publications, 1981

Myers M: Angry, abandoned husbands: assessment and treatment. Unpublished paper, Department of Psychiatry, Shaunessy Hospital, Vancouver, British Columbia, 1983

Neidig P: Attitudinal characteristics of males who have engaged in spouse abuse. Paper presented at the Second National Conference for Family Violence Researchers, University of New Hampshire, Durham, August 1982

Novaco R: Anger and coping with stress: cognitive-behavioral interventions, in Cognitive Behavior Therapy: Research and Applications. Edited by Foreyt J, Rathjen D. New York, Plenum Press, 1978

Phillips C, Derman-Sparks L: Becoming anti-racist: patterns and progressions of change for whites and people of color. Paper presented at the American Orthopsychiatric Association's annual meeting, Boston, April 1982

Rich A: On Lies, Secrets, and Silence. New York, Norton, 1979

Rimm D: Treatment of anti-social aggression, in Treatment of Human Problems: A Social Learning Approach. Edited by Harris G. New York, Grune & Stratton, 1977

Roy M. Battered Women: A Psychosocial Study of Domestic Violence. New York, Van Nostrand Reinhold, 1977

Schechter S: Women and Male Violence: The Visions and Struggles of the Battered Women's Movement. Boston, South End Press, 1982

Sonkin D, Durphy M: Learning to Live Without Violence. San Francisco, Volcano Press, 1982

Strauss M, Gelles R, Steinmetz S: Behind Closed Doors: Violence in the American Family. Garden City, NY, Anchor Press/Doubleday, 1980

Walker L: The Battered Woman. New York, Harper & Row, 1979

Warrior B: Working on Wife-Abuse (Seventh Supplemental Edition). Cambridge, MA, Women's Center, 1978

Wilson-Schaef A: Women's Reality: An Emerging Female System in the White Male Society. Minneapolis, Winston Press, 1981

Chapter 6

Elder Neglect, Abuse, and Exploitation

MARION ZUCKER GOLDSTEIN, M.D.

Chapter 6

Elder Neglect, Abuse, and Exploitation

November 1940, Prins Hendriklaan 28, Amsterdam, Holland: German occupation troops with their ominous high black military boots kick the elderly down the elegantly carpeted stairs of a Jewish Home for the Aged, tear off wigs, shout humiliations, threaten, intimidate, and demand to have their orders carried out beyond the physical and emotional endurance of their victims. At 1:00 A.M. this group of Jewish elderly, made destitute overnight, with their Jewish caregivers, were marched to a "gathering place" where they had to stand in line under threat of being gunned down if anyone would turn his or her head while awaiting deportation to places unknown. It was an unforgettable scene for a nine-year-old, now this chapter's author.

Abuse sanctioned by government is indeed a manifestation of abysmal deprivation, especially when we consider the fact that the "civilized" world was unable or not inclined to stop it in a timely fashion.

The above example leaves no doubt in our minds about the use of the expression "elder abuse," by governmental edict no less. How does that relate to our current use of the term and current governmental involvement in the protection and care of the vulnerable elderly? Mandatory reporting laws concerning child abuse first evolved in the 1960s; spouse abuse laws followed 10 years later. Only in the late 1970s did our government begin to pay attention to elder abuse, neglect, and exploitation as forms of family violence that needed to be addressed by reporting laws and protective interventions (Taler and Ansello 1985).

Estimates suggest that 500,000 to 1.5 million cases of abuse, neglect, or exploitation of the elderly occur annually in the United States (U.S. Senate and the Select Committee

101

on Aging 1980). Elder abuse is difficult to document since abuser and victim tend to deny and minimize its seriousness (Goldstein and Blank 1982). This is not surprising since 80 percent of home care to the aged is given by family members living in the same household, and one-third of these elderly persons require constant care (Shanas 1979).

It is estimated that four percent of the nation's elderly population are victims of some form of abuse, yet only one-sixth of the cases of elder abuse comes to the authorities' attention (Gardner and Halamandaris 1981). Some estimate that as many as one-fourth of the elderly who live with their families may suffer from abuse or neglect at some time (Kosberg 1983). Neglect of a passive nature, that is, inattention or isolation, has been shown to be by far the most common form of elder abuse (Kosberg 1983; Block and Sinnott 1979). Studies indicate that many victims are chronically abused. One study reported that previous incidents of abuse had occurred in 58 percent of cases (Kosberg 1983); another study found that abuse was repetitive in about 70 percent of cases (Hickey and Douglas 1981).

Physical, verbal, emotional, and financial abuse, neglect, or exploitation of the elderly have been found to occur in families in which the now-adult children were raised with abuse. In addition, pathology in one or more family members including drug and/or alcohol abuse is common. Probably the most frequent etiology of abuse is from an imbalance of the needs of the elderly and resources available to meet these needs. When an elder is victimized, many patterns of family violence exist. One may question at times who is victimized—the obvious victims or the caregiver with limited physical, emotional, and/or financial resources, who willingly or by default assumes the responsibility for the dependent elder who is no longer held responsible for his or her behavior? Physical and mental impairment of the elderly can be harmful to the caregivers when the former's dependency needs outweigh the caregivers' capacity to give and family and community resources are either lacking or insufficient.

Throughout the literature review to follow, the author would like the reader to keep in mind that the professional, institution, or agency who detects the problem of elder abuse, neglect, or exploitation must conceptualize the entire situation in order not to perpetuate the problem by being overwhelmed and pointing a finger at the often overstressed caregiver. Most often the caregiver is a middle-aged woman (Brody 1979) whose caregiving and self-sacrificing have brought her to exhaustion. She as well should be offered supports and resources rather than be cast aside as an "elder abuser." With the increase in frail elderly in our population, burnout of caregiving has to be detected at every level and should not stop at the level of the professional person. The supports available or unavailable to the professional person who does the reporting must also be assessed. Once elder abuse, neglect, or exploitation has been reported, what we do to improve the quality of life of the elderly and their caregivers must be addressed (O'Malley et al. 1979). We must ask ourselves why it is so often that caregiver and elderly stay in a disastrously stressful situation over prolonged periods of time. Is it not that the alternative of lack of privacy and familiar surroundings, institutional herding, and stripping of all individuality seem as grim as the humiliations experienced in an abusive, neglectful, or exploitive home situation? Ralph Nader's statement 17 years ago has not been improved upon:

> The conventional injustices of the land bear down heavily on the elderly. Consumer fraud, inflation, fixed pensions. . . . But more gnawing and omnipresent is the psychological devastation heaped on the old . . . they are no longer wanted, they are no longer useful . . . in short they are considered a drag. There is a colossal collective callousness that pervades society. . . . The most intense focus of what has been wrought for old people is the nursing home. (Towsend 1971)

A literature review 17 years later by the American Psychiatric Association's Council on the Aging Task Force on Nursing Homes will verify this tragedy, which has been modified only by the existence of an occasional "model teaching nursing home" (unpublished report).

Definition of Terms

The definition of elder abuse varies widely, depending on the researcher who is collecting data. Several efforts have been made to standardize the language and to devise the screening instrument. The Elder Abuse Prevention, Identification and Treatment Act of 1985, H.R. 1674, introduced by Senator Claude Pepper (D-Fla.) and modeled after the Child Abuse Act of 1974, defines abuse, exploitation, neglect, and physical harm as follows:

> The term *abuse* means the willful infliction of injury, unreasonable confinement, intimidation or cruel punishment with resulting physical harm or pain or mental anguish; or the willful deprivation by a caretaker of goods or services which are necessary to avoid harm, mental anguish or mental illness. The term *exploitation* means the illegal or improper act or process of a caretaker using the resources of an elder for monetary or personal benefit, profit or gain. The term *neglect* means the failure to provide . . . the goods or services which are necessary to avoid physical harm, mental anguish or mental illness or the failure of a caregiver to provide such goods or services. The term *physical harm* means bodily pain, injury, impairment or disease. (U.S. Congress 1985)

The Elder Assessment Instrument (EAI) was developed over a four-year period at Boston's Beth Israel Hospital (Fulmer et al. 1984; Fulmer and Wetle 1986) and was determined to be valid ($r = .83$) and reliable ($r = .83$). The categories covered in this instrument are the areas mandated to be reported: physical abuse, neglect, mental anguish, and exploitation. The EAI also evaluates the level of dependency that can be used in assessing the caregiver's ability and resources to handle the elderly's needs as well

TABLE 1. Elder Assessment

Date _____ Person completing form _____
Payment status (check one): _____ BlueCross/Blue Shield
_____ Medicaid _____ Medicare _____ Private Payment
_____ Other
Residence (check one): _____ Home
_____ Name of nursing home
_____ Other (e.g., son's/daughter's home)

Accompanied by: _____ Family _____ Friend _____ Alone
_____ Nursing home personnel
Reason for visit: _____ Cardiac _____ Changed mental status
_____ Fall _____ G.I. _____ Orthopedic
_____ Other (specify) _____
Current mental status: _____ Oriented
_____ Confused _____ Unresponsive

1) **General Assessment**	Very good	Good	Undecided	Poor	Very poor	No basis for judgment
a) Clothing						
b) Hygiene						
c) Nutrition						
d) Skin integrity						

Additional comments: _____
_____
_____
_____
_____
_____
_____
_____
_____
_____
_____
_____
_____
_____

TABLE 1. Elder Assessment *(continued)*

2) **Physical Assessment**	Definite evidence	Probable evidence	Uncertain	Probably no evidence	No evidence	No basis for judgment
a) Bruising						
b) Contractures						
c) Decubiti						
d) Dehydration						
e) Diarrhea						
f) Impaction						
g) Lacerations						
h) Malnutrition						
i) Urine burns/excoriations						

Additional comments: _____

_____

_____

_____

_____

3) **Usual Lifestyle**	Totally independent	Mostly independent	Uncertain	Mostly dependent	Totally dependent	No basis for judgment
a) Administration of medications						
b) Ambulation						
c) Continence						
d) Feedings						
e) Maintenance of hygiene						
f) Management of finances						
g) Family involvement						

Additional comments: _____

_____

_____

_____

_____

_____

TABLE 1. Elder Assessment *(continued)*

4) Social Assessment

a) Narrative statement regarding patient-identified social problems: _____

_____

_____

_____

_____

b) Family/nursing home perception of problem: _____

_____

_____

_____

	Very good quality	Good quality	Uncertain	Poor quality	Very poor quality	No basis for judgment
c) Financial situation						
d) Interaction with family						
e) Interaction with friends						
f) Interaction with nursing home personnel						
g) Living arrangement						
h) Observed relationship with care provider						
i) Participation in daily social activities						
j) Support systems						
k) Ability to express needs						

Additional comments: (recent changes in life situation) _____

_____

_____

_____

_____

_____

_____

_____

TABLE 1. Elder Assessment *(continued)*

	Definite evidence	Evidence	Possibility	Probably no evidence	No evidence	No basis/ not applicable
5) Medical Assessment						
a) Duplication of similar medications (e.g., multiple laxatives, sedatives)						
b) Unusual doses of medication						
c) Alcohol/substance abuse						
d) Greater than 15-percent dehydration						
e) Bruises and/or fractures beyond what is compatible with alleged trauma						
f) Failure to respond to warning of obvious disease						
g) Repetitive admissions due to probable failure of health care surveillance						

(Attach description of any additional physical findings)

Additional comments: (Note: if either 5a or 5b has been answered in the affirmative, please elaborate and be **as specific as possible**)

_____

_____

_____

_____

_____

_____

_____

_____

TABLE 1. Elder Assessment *(continued)*

	Definite evidence	Evidence	Possibility	Probably no evidence	No evidence	No basis/not applicable
6) Summary Assessments						
a) Evidence of financial/ possession abuse						
b) Evidence of physical abuse						
c) Evidence of psychological abuse						
d) History of recent life crisis						

Additional comments: _____

_____

_____

_____

	Yes	No
7) Disposition		
a) Referral to elder assessment team		
b) Referral to clinical advisor		

8) General Comments: (Nursing home contact person and today's date) ____

_____

_____

_____

_____

_____

_____

_____

_____

_____

_____

_____

Reprinted with permission from Fulmer T, Wetle T: Elder abuse screening and intervention. Nurse Pract 11:36-37, 1986.

as the need for psychiatric and other medical services and social work interventions.

Elder Assessment

Research has been recommended in the area of 1) detecting risk factors for abuse within the family setting, 2) determining which interventions might minimize these factors, and 3) assessing the impact as well as cost of interventions (Rathbone-McCuan 1980; Rathbone-McCuan and Hashimi 1982; Rathbone-McCuan and Voyles 1982; Rathbone-McCuan et al. 1983). This is both a step beyond the mere detection of abuse symptoms after they have occurred and a step toward prevention.

No legal definitions or checklist instruments can surpass a detailed assessment of the physical and mental condition and dependency level of the elderly. A sensitive interview of the caregiver, during which stresses and conflicts are revealed, behaviors to deal with them explored, and open expression facilitated, cannot and should not be replaced by objective instrument assessments. In the long run, sound reality-based recommendations and actions to alleviate the stresses and to resolve conflict could be more helpful than reporting.

As a nation we tend to contribute to the adversarial stance out of which profiles of abuser and victim have evolved. As a society our code of behavior reveals an abusing, neglectful society at large, struggling ever so slowly to improve the situation by firm efforts at mandatory reporting, feeble efforts at protecting, and almost no efforts to assure optimal quality of life.

The Legal System

Most states have their own mandatory reporting laws for elder abuse; however, some states have none, and others are still giving the matter consideration. The number of states that require health care professionals to report abuse of older adults by family members has doubled from 16 in 1981 (Rathbone-McCuan and Voyles 1982) to 37 in 1986 (Salend et al. 1984). In most of these 37 states, the purpose of the statutes is to create a statewide protective service system. Some states also mandate reporting of abuse of developmentally disabled adults and general domestic violence though none have penalties for not reporting. Twenty-seven statutes include psychologic abuse such as mental anguish, 28 include exploitation of another person, and 34 include neglect (Gilbert 1986). Self-neglect, that is, failure of older adults to provide essentials for themselves, is expressly included in 20 statutes (Gilbert 1986), occasionally, statutes also specify unreasonable confinement, cruel punishment, and abandonment. The older adults' wishes are not taken into consideration in most statutes, and health professionals are required to report cases where they have reason to suspect elder abuse. In California, health professionals must have actual knowledge of abuse before they are mandated to report it (Gilbert 1986). These reports are to be made to a state or local agency. After the investigation, the agency is authorized to provide or arrange for protective services in all but five states (Gilbert 1986).

When reports are made in good faith, health professionals are immune from both civil and criminal liability in 29 states and from civil liability in 7 states (Gilbert 1986). Twenty-six of the 32 statutes that mention providing protective services specifically state that services are not to be provided without the consent of the abused person (Gilbert 1986). Studies suggest that 40 percent of older adults whom health care professionals believed were abused refused intervention of services (O'Malley et al. 1983). If the older person lacks the capacity to consent, the state has the power to protect those helpless to protect themselves and to protect society by restricting the self-determination of people who inflict harm (Horstman 1975).

Autonomy in the form of consent to services is addressed in many statutes, but there is no agreement on what it means

111

to lack capacity to consent. Psychiatrists have established criteria for competence (Roth et al. 1977), but courts have disagreed (Kapp 1981). Though 26 of the mandatory reporting statutes mention consent to protective services, none mention consent to reports being filed. Only Alaska, California, New Mexico, and Tennessee request consent of the older person to the agency investigation subsequent to the reporting of abuse (Gilbert 1986). As seen in Table 2, statutes vary from state to state and those that focus on the elderly imply a level of incompetence where self-determination on the part of the elderly can be overlooked because of age. The fact that the elder abuse statutes are based on child abuse statutes tends to confirm the assumption and bias that the elderly are like immature children.

There is much room for reflection and reconsideration here. Whereas patients are entitled to refuse medical treatment despite the fact that such refusal may end in death, both the mandatory reporting system and the protective service system imply that persons reported are not entitled to make choices regarding personal eating habits, dress, cleanliness, or other elements that we term self- or other neglect when not attended to (Katz 1980).

Autonomy of the elderly is often curtailed under the guise of caregiving. There is a delicate balance between maintaining as high a level of autonomy, dignity, and self-esteem as feasible while limitations of physical and functional capacity persist, and this frequently tends to be overlooked in decision making on behalf of the dependent elderly. Ten years ago in Great Britain a consulting psychiatrist questioned nursing practices that impinged on the importance of life for the older person when it meant unnecessary pain and loss of dignity (Baker 1977). He also questioned whether self-neglecting elderly in the community are better or worse off than if they are placed in the hospital for medical treatment where privacy and sense of dignity are so often lost (Baker 1976).

Profiles of Abused Elderly and Their Caregivers

Numerous studies of varying quality have been undertaken to shed light on who reports what kind of elder abuse, who the persons are who perpetrate the elder abuse, the nature of the abuse, the nature of previous victim impairment, and the impairment following the abuse. Correlation studies are rare and numbers of each variable relatively small in each study. In most surveys the list of recommendations is uniformly thorough and extensive (Johnson 1985). Studies agree that lack of adequate resources most frequently leads to abuse of the elderly regardless of the profile of the abuser and the victim. In other words, the questions of who does what to whom, when, and under what circumstances are far from answered. Thus far surveys and research have been rather fragmented because of difficulties in identification, the complexity of the problems, and reluctance of funding agencies to fund long-term studies. The profiles that have evolved to date are as yet scattered but are nonetheless revealing. It has been concluded that the violence between adult members of a household and their older relatives is different from other forms of family violence and that long-range epidemiologic studies are needed (Block 1981).

Demographics

Available information reveals that the majority of victims were found to be females over 75 who did not have sufficient income to live independently (Block and Sinnott 1979; O'Malley et al. 1979; Lau and Kosberg 1979). Some studies have shown that victims have one or more physical or mental impairments that preclude adequate self-care and independent living (Pillemer and Wolf 1983).

Though abuse of the elderly presumably crosses racial, socioeconomic, and ethnic backgrounds (Steuer and Austin 1980), some studies show trends that appear to depend on the population or area studied. The Michigan Institute of

113

TABLE 2. Reporting Requirements by State

State	Age Specified	Immediate Report Necessary (Physical mistreatment, mental anguish, neglect and exploitation are reported unless noted otherwise.)	Reportable Abuse Events
Alabama	18+	X	
Alaska	65+	Within 24 hours	Except mental anguish
Arizona	18+	X	
Arkansas	65+	X	
California	65+	X	Except mental anguish
Colorado	65+	X	
Connecticut	60+	Within 5 days	Only exploitation
Delaware	18+	X	
Florida		X	
Georgia	18+		Except exploitation
Hawaii	65+	X	
Idaho	60+	Within 24 hours	Except mental anguish and neglect
Illinois	60+		Except mental anguish
Iowa	18+		
Kentucky	18+	X	
Louisiana	18+	X	
Maine	18+	X	
Massachusetts	60+	X	
Michigan	18+	X	Except exploitation
Minnesota	18+	X	Only physical mistreatment
Missouri	18+	X	

State	Age		Notes
Montana	60+		Only physical mistreatment and neglect
Nebraska	60+	X	Except mental anguish
Nevada	60+	X	Except mental anguish
New Hampshire	18+	"Promptly"	
New Mexico	55+		Except mental anguish
N. Carolina	18+		
Ohio	60+	X	Except physical mistreatment and neglect
Oklahoma	65+	"Promptly"	Except mental anguish
Oregon	65+	X	Except mental anguish
Rhode Island	60+	X	
South Carolina	18+	X	
Tennessee	18+	X	
Texas	65+		Except mental anguish
Utah	18+	X	Except mental anguish
Vermont	60+	X	
Virginia	18+	X	
Washington	60+	X	Only physical mistreatment and neglect
West Virginia	18+	X	Except mental anguish
Wisconsin	60+		Except mental anguish
Wyoming			

Adapted from Thobaben, Marshelle and Anderson, Linda: "Reporting Elder Abuse: It's the Law," AJN, April 1985, pp. 371-4. Thobaben and Anderson are both associate professors in the department of nursing at Humboldt State University, Arcata, Calif.

Reprinted with permission from Fulmer T, Wetle T: Elder abuse screening and interventions. *Nurse Pract* 11:36-37, 1986.

Gerontology study found a lower class profile (Department of Health, Education and Welfare 1980), and the University of Maryland Center on Aging study showed a middle and lower class profile (Block and Sinnott 1979). Again, depending on which groups are studied, degree of physical and/or mental impairment varies. One study found significantly greater degrees of mental impairment in orientation and memory in a group of physically abused elderly whose increase in dependency had occurred shortly before the reported abuse (Pillemer and Wolf 1983). In this author's clinical experience, with laudable exceptions, the lack of accurate assessment of the level of dementia and functional impairment is rampant. This leads to unrealistic expectations of the demented elderly and an extraordinary sense of frustration on the part of the caregiver with the actual level of dependence requiring him or her to take on ever more chores.

Though elaborate instruments for assessment are used in well-funded research protocols, clinical application and well-trained staff are often lacking to assist the elderly and their caregivers because of inadequate Medicare reimbursement to carry out the needed evaluation and to render appropriate treatment. Though a national program, Medicare reimbursement varies from state to state and region to region. Care available in one region of the country is not reimbursed in another. A case in point is the length of stay in a psychiatric hospital afforded the demented and/or depressed elderly in western Pennsylvania and the variety of community placements available. Comparable care is lacking in western New York where Medicare has been known to disallow hospital workup and treatment with regularity after 14 days, and families are made to take their relatives home regardless of unbearable stresses because of state regulations mandating that no more institutional settings be made available until 1991.

The New York State policies promote rather than alleviate elder abuse by state edicts that do not take the realities of the dependent elderly and their caregivers into consideration. *If a generalization can be made about any one profile of abusive caregivers, it is that there is a lack of adequate resources to help care for their dependent elderly.* The level of resistance to care on the part of the elderly has been observed and commented on repeatedly but has not been effectively correlated with abuse (Taler and Ansello 1985). The perpetrators of abuse are often spouses, themselves elderly and needy, or an unmarried, unemployed child, often a daughter over 50, who have provided caregiving for a decade or longer (Johnson 1985). One statewide reporting system revealed that perpetrators of abuse with alcohol and other psychiatric problems were the minority of those studied (Walker 1983). It may be speculated that the pathology was acquired in the course of the unrelenting demands of caregiving (Drinka and Smith 1983).

Past intra- and intergenerational conflicts and behaviors bear heavily on present conduct and have been shown consistently to contribute to the profile of *abuser* and *victim* (Johnson 1985; Wilks 1981; Stauss et al. 1980).

Many studies deal with physical abuse of the elderly since it is more observable and can be dealt with more concretely. No measurement of mental anguish or exploitation has been established except for the most obvious and blatant situations. Even those instances are relative and depend on how they are perceived by the supposedly unbiased observer.

Protective Services Legislation

So what are we doing about abuse, neglect, and exploitation of the elderly, other than identifying and studying the problems, which is indeed a commendable beginning? After several trials and tribulations, we now have Public Law 98-457, which calls for the establishment of a Federal Family Violence Center that would include elder abuse. We also have a Model Adult Protective Services Act, prepared by the Senate Select Committee on Aging, to provide guidelines for

117

states in the development and implementation of elder neglect and abuse legislation. These acts authorize the least restrictive and appropriate forms of intervention, preferably on a voluntary basis, but with the possibility of involuntary participation. A wide range of services will be provided to assist the elderly in maintaining an independent lifestyle that will presumably invite their cooperation. This general philosophy has the potential to do a disservice to the frail, dependent elderly if monies are diverted in such a way that hospitals and other community caregiving settings cannot develop adequate numbers of well-trained staff.

Participation of the Medical Profession

Nurses and social workers were the first to be actively involved in the identification and treatment of cases perceived as "elder abuse" as evidenced by their early numerous publications. More recently, the American Medical Association's (AMA's) Council on Scientific Affairs has reviewed nine major publications on elder abuse from the last six years and summarized elder abuse of the following types: abuse (physical, psychological, sexual), exploitation (financial, material), neglect (active, that is physical; passive, that is, psychological), self-neglect, violation of rights, and medical (Council on Scientific Affairs 1987). The Washington State Medical Association classified these categories into more detail (see Table 3).

In a further effort to provide guidelines for physicians, a model bill known as the Elderly Abuse Reporting Act, prepared by the AMA Department of State Legislation, was created. This model bill reads as follows:

"Abuse" shall mean an act or omission which results in harm or threatened harm to the health or welfare of an elderly person. Abuse includes intentional infliction of physical or mental injury, sexual abuse, or withholding of necessary food, clothing and medical care to meet the physical and mental

TABLE 3. Classification of Types of Elder Abuse

Physical or sexual abuse
Bruises (bilateral and at different stages of healing) Welts
Lacerations
Punctures
Fractures
Evidence of excessive drugging
Burns
Physical constraints (tying to beds, etc.)
Malnutrition and/or dehydration
Lack of personal care
Inadequate heating
Lack of food and water
Unclean clothes and bedding
Lack of needed medication
Lack of eyeglasses, hearing aids, false teeth
Difficulty in walking or sitting
Venereal disease
Pain or itching, bruises, or bleeding of external genitalia, vaginal area, or anal area

Psychological abuse (vulnerable adults react by exhibiting resignation, fear, depression, mental confusion, anger, ambivalence, insomnia)
Threats
Insults
Harassment
Withholding of security and affection
Harsh orders
Refusal on the part of the family or those caring for the adult to allow travel, visits by friends or other family members, or attendance at religious observances

119

TABLE 3. Classification of Types of Elder Abuse *(continued)*

Exploitation
Misuse of vulnerable adult's income or other financial resources (victim is best source of information, but in most cases has turned management of financial affairs over to another person; as a result, there may be some confusion about finances)

Medical abuse
Withholding or improper administration of medications or necessary medical treatments for a condition, or the withholding of aids the person would medically require such as false teeth, glasses, hearing aids
May be a cause of
   Confusion
   Disorientation
   Memory impairment
   Agitation
   Lethargy
   Self-neglect

Neglect
Conduct of vulnerable adult or others that results in deprivation of care necessary to maintain physical and mental health
May be manifested by
   Malnutrition
   Poor personal hygiene
   Any of the indicators for medical abuse

Reprinted from Council on Scientific Affairs: Elder abuse and neglect. JAMA 257:966-971, 1987. Copyright 1987, American Medical Association.

health needs of an elderly person by one having the care, custody or responsibility of an elderly person. (American Medical Association 1985).

With these guidelines for the medical profession, it remains up to each specialty to define their particular role and participation in the multidisciplinary efforts it takes to address the issues of elder abuse which have been described by the U.S. House of Representatives Select Committee on Aging (1981) as "alien to the American ideal." This system when adequately funded and an integral part of a broader system, has the potential to diminish elder abuse.

Conclusion

The suggested legislation recommends establishment of a protective service system using grants from federal, state, and other public and private sources to support the system. It also sets forth the powers and duties of a state agency responsible for organizing a protective service system. The legislation suggests that the protective services are part of a broader program but that the target population remains the infirm, incapacitated elderly on whose behalf the protective system can only intervene with court authorization if the elderly under consideration do not consent. Elderly persons who wish to receive protective services and can afford to pay are eligible to receive them. Emergency orders for protective services are explicitly described and involuntary placement has to be followed by a court hearing within 48 hours of involuntary placement, which is not to last longer than 6 months at a time without a renewed hearing. Placement cannot be changed unless the court authorizes a transfer of residence for compelling reasons. The elderly person is entitled to counsel and independent evaluation at his or her own or state expense and to be present at the hearing unless physically or mentally incapacitated. This system certainly cannot replace adequate Medicare reimbursement for appropriate physical and mental health care for the elderly and their caregivers on a more uniform national basis so that environment, staffing patterns, and training can be addressed in acute and long-term care settings. If we report instead of service, if we insist on independence when care is needed, we do not yet protect where protection is needed.

References

American Medical Association: Model Elderly Abuse Reporting Act. Chicago, IL, American Medical Association, 1985

Baker AA: Granny battering. Nurs Mirror 144(8):65–66, 1977

Baker AA: Slow euthanasia—or "she will be better off in hospital." Br Med J 2:571–572, 1976

Block MR: "Elder abuse research issues for the future." First National Conference on Abuse of Older Persons, Cambridge, MA, March 1981, Conference Proceedings, Boston, MA, March 1981, Legal Research and Services for the Elderly, 1981

Block MR, Sinnott JD (eds): The Battered Elder Syndrome: An Exploratory Study. College Park, MD, University of Maryland Center on Aging, 1979

Brody E: Women's changing roles: the aging family and long-term care of older people. National JT 11:1828–33, 1979

Council on Scientific Affairs–AMA Council Report: Elder abuse and neglect. JAMA 257:966–971, 1987

Department of Health, Education and Welfare: Battered Elderly: a Hidden Problem. Washington, DC, Department of Health, Education and Welfare, 1980

Drinka T, Smith J: Depression in caregivers of demented patients (abstract). Gerontologist 116, 1983

Fulmer T, Wetle T: Elder abuse screening and intervention. Nurse Pract 11:33–38, 1986

Fulmer T, et al. Abuse of the elderly: screening and detection. J Emerg Nurs 10:131–140, 1984

Gardner K, Halamandaris VJ: Elder abuse (an examination of a hidden problem): a report with additional views by the Select Committee on Aging. U.S. House of Representatives 97th Congress, Washington, DC, U.S. Government Printing Office, 1981

Gilbert AD: The ethics of mandatory elder abuse reporting statutes. Advances in Nursing Science 51–62, 1986

Goldstein SE, Blank A: The elderly: abused or abuser? Can Med Assoc J 127:455–456, 1982

Hickey T, Douglas RL: Mistreatment of the elderly in the domestic setting: an exploratory study. Am J Public Health 71:500–507, 1981

Horstman PM: Protective services for the elderly: the limits of parens patriae. Missouri Law Review 40:215–278, 1975

Johnson T, O'Brien J, Hudson MF: Elder Neglect and Abuse: An Annotated Bibliography. Westport, CT, Greenwood Press, 1985

Kapp MB: Legal guardianship. Geriatric Nursing 2:366–369, 1981

Katz KD: Elder abuse. Journal of Family Law 18:695–722, 1980

Kosberg JL (ed): Abuse and Maltreatment of the Elderly. Boston, MA, Wright-PSG, 1983

Lau E, Kosberg JJI: Abuse of the elderly by informal care providers. Aging 1979

O'Malley H, Segel H, Perez R: Elder Abuse in Massachusetts: A Survey of Professionals and Paraprofessionals. Boston, MA, Legal Research and Services for the Elderly, 1979

O'Malley TA, Everitt DE, O'Malley HC, et al: Identifying and preventing family-mediated abuse and neglect of elderly persons. Ann Intern Med 98:998–1005, 1983

Pillemer KA, Wolf RS: The role of dependency in physical abuse of the elderly (abstract). Gerontologist 312, 1983

Rathbone-McCuan E: Elderly victims of family violence and neglect. Soc Casework 61:296–304, 1980

Rathbone-McCuan E, Hashimi J (eds): Elder abuse and isolation: isolated elders. Health and Social Intervention 177–209 Rockville, MD, Aspen Systems Corp., 1982

Rathbone-McCuan E, Voyles B: Case detection of abused elderly parents. Am J Psychiatry 139:189–192, 1982

Rathbone-McCuan E, Travis A, Voyles B: Family intervention: the task-centered approach, in Abuse and Maltreatment of the Elderly: Causes and Interventions. Edited by Kosberg JL. Littleton, MA, John Wright PSG, 1983

Roth LH, Meisle A, Lidz CW: Tests of competency to consent to treatment. Am J Psychiatry 134:279–284, 1977

Salend E, Kane RA, Satz FM, et al: Elder abuse reporting: limitation of statutes. Gerontologist 24:61–69, 1984

Shanas E: Social myth as hypothesis: the case of the family relations of older people. Gerontologist 19:3–9, 1979

Stauss MA, Gelles RJ, Steinmetz SK: Behind Closed Doors: Violence in the American Family. Garden City, NJ, Anchor Press/Doubleday, 1980

Steuer J, Austin E: Family abuse of the elderly. J Am Geriatr Soc 28:372–376, 1980

Taler G, Ansello E: Elder abuse. AFP 32:107–114, 1985

Towsend C: The Nader Report: Old Age, the Last Segregation. New York, Grossman Publishers, 1971

U.S. Congress: Joint Hearings before the Special Committee on Aging. U.S. Senate and the Select Committee on Aging, U.S. House of Representatives 96th Congress, Washington, DC, 1980

U.S. Congress, House: The Elder Abuse Prevention, Identification and Treatment Act. H.R. 1674, 1985

Walker JC: Protective services for the elderly: Connecticut's experience, in Abuse and Maltreatment of the Elderly: Causes and Interventions. Edited by Kosberg JI. Littleton, MA, John Wright PSG, 1983

Washington State Medical Association: Elder Abuse Guidelines for Intervention by Physicians and Other Service Providers. Seattle, WA, Washington State Medical Association, 1985

Wilks C: Past conflict and current stress: factors in the abuse of the elderly, in Proceedings of the Tennessee Conference on Abuse of Older Persons. Knoxville, TN, School of Social Work, Office of Continuing Social Work Education, 1981

Chapter 7

Domestic Violence and the Police: Theory, Policy, and Practice

PETER J. MANCUSO, JR.

Chapter 7

Domestic Violence and the Police: Theory, Policy, and Practice

Since entering a career in law enforcement 18 years ago, I have come to view police activities around domestic violence as perhaps the most important among the wide array of duties performed by our officers. This transition in thinking evolved over time as it has for many law enforcement officials. However, many more have not come to terms with domestic violence. For them, it remains a difficult and unwelcome issue.

The History of Family Law

How volatile the issue can become is better understood by examining the history of law and the family in western society. Since the rise of civilization in Europe (the cradle of our own legal system), family law has stood apart from both the criminal and civil codes. Indeed, in Roman times, family law constituted a separate and distinct portion of the Roman legal system and gave absolute authority to the male head of the household. The husband/father of Roman times could admonish other household members including children and wife, and in certain circumstances this authority extended to include capital punishment.

This distinction between family law and criminal and civil law has largely prevailed down through the centuries. It has survived the fall of the Roman Empire, the rise and decline of feudalism, the Renaissance, and the Age of Enlightenment. It was transported to our shores with the early settlers from Europe, where it soon became part of our own

127

legal traditions, and wasn't challenged until the mid-19th century. Then an attempt to shelter a child from abuse at home led the rescuers to the Society for the Prevention of Cruelty to Animals as their only recourse. Soon, a Society for the Prevention of Cruelty to Children was created. This represented the first serious attempt to deal with that portion of domestic violence that we recognize today as child abuse. This organization, and others modeled after it, were greatly aided by both the compulsory education and child labor laws that were springing up at the turn of the century. However, despite these relatively progressive times, domestic violence, particularly violence between spouses, went largely unnoticed and unchecked. Even the women's suffrage movement did little to influence the legal treatment of the family. Instead, external evils, such as alcohol or gambling, were seen as the cause of many social problems, including an abusive father or husband.

During this same period, the western world saw the rise of criminology. Amazingly, criminology, through its many evolutionary phases, the positive school, the neo-positive, the psychologic, the sociologic, and the radical, has largely bypassed the family. This is true in terms of both crime as a phenomenon within the family and crime as an outgrowth of family violence. Only the sociologic school placed an emphasis on the family—the broken family, that is. This post-World War II school has greatly influenced law enforcement executives right up to the modern era. The value that any family is better than a broken family transcends mere criminology, however, and remains today a potent social value despite other shifting forces, including sexual norms, divorce laws, and even the dual income economy.

This view was greatly helped along by that mover and shaker of values—television. Up until the last decade, American television amplified and enhanced the image of the American family as a caring, sheltering, loving institution composed of legally and properly married parents raising mischievous, but properly acquired children. Even within the last decade, despite television's attempts to depict family settings outside the traditional family structure, television's family life remains a situation comedy. When drama is the milieu, even that stalwart of television drama, the police story, rarely commits the taboo of dealing with family violence. This, despite the fact that long ago story lines were created that dealt with rape and incest. The good old family fight still remains, for the most part, a taboo for television producers, and when they do work up the interest to deal with domestic violence, they lean toward the sensational, for example, "The Burning Bed."

Family Disputes

Throughout the naiveté of early television, while Ralph was threatening to send Alice "to the moon" on the Honeymooners, family problems, specifically violence, were beginning to manifest themselves upon the legal system so much so that in places like New York State, the Family Court was being converted from the old Juvenile Court. This court would be supported by the state's department of probation, which was directly in vogue with the sociological view of criminology. That family court would be a civil court and would deploy social agencies and social workers (in the form of probation officers) "to help preserve the family."

During this time of transition from the mid-1950s through the late 1960s, two phenomena were steadfastly at play: crime was increasing, and the criminal justice system was falling behind. Within this environment both the propensity and mandate for police to use the family courts were overwhelming. As trial time was abated, prosecutors and court administrators developed formal and informal rules to refer almost all violence within the family to family court. Therefore, family crime, some of it quite brutal, became almost exclusively a civil matter, though not the torts or divorce variety of civil law, but rather the medical model of civil law. This model attempted to heal the family: victims, offenders, and bystanders alike, often making little, if any, distinction among the three.

Family Courts

With the family courts came the first large-scale deployment of police policy around domestic violence issues. That policy reflected the formal and informal policies of court administrators and prosecutors alike. It should be understood that within almost every political–judicial–governmental jurisdiction, the police are at the bottom of that structure and it is the rare situation at any level of government in the United States when the police drive criminal justice policy. Therefore, police policy meant greater use of family courts.

Of course, this policy had some inherent problems that quickly revealed themselves. First and foremost was the fact that the combination of increased juvenile delinquency and the police policy of referring more matters to family court quickly overwhelmed the new judicial system (the family court in almost all jurisdictions handles juvenile delinquency matters). Second, the family court, although deploying a medical model of treatment, had very few resources at its disposal. Offender treatment programs, victim advocacy groups, and women's shelters were at least a decade in the future, while divorce was still a huge undertaking, both socially and legally. Finally, little noticed, except by the victims themselves, was the fact that family courts did little to make the family environment a safer place. It would take bold legal action, backed by the huge social groundswell of women's rights, to bring that fact to light a decade later.

Police Policy in the Mid to Late 1960s

Theoretically family disputes were best handled outside the purview of criminal law, deploying instead social resources secured through the new courts. The policy was that family disputes should be handled by the family court except in the

130

most serious matters like homicide and attempted homicide. The actual practice was that police brought before the family court through arrest, but more often through referral, enough cases to saturate the new court system. The police in turn adjusted their style to help the system cope, not only with the problems of the courts, but also with the problems they, themselves, were facing: growing crime, subsequent growing arrests, and growing calls for service as a result of better communications technology. Family disputes were most often handled by threats to the offender to "knock it off" and to "take a walk" or "get a hotel room for the night." Of course, sometimes these threats developed into assaults on the officers by one or both parties, which in turn resulted in an embarrassing arrest by the officer and occasionally, an injury or even death of the officer or one of the family members.

Family Crisis Intervention

The prevailing conditions just described existed for most police officers in the United States by the late 1960s and were certainly the conditions for America's urban police officers. It was within this situation, and the problems that were inherent in this setting, that great hope was placed in a theory called family crisis intervention (FCI).

FCI was the work of Dr. Morton Bard, psychologist and former police officer (Bard 1970). Although Bard had been away from policing nearly 20 years when he proposed FCI in 1967, he still had a keen sense of the human problems encountered by police officers and how modern psychology might be deployed by officers to help them accomplish their missions.

Crisis intervention itself was born in the wake of a terrible tragedy, the Coconut Grove nightclub fire. On that dreadful evening in the early 1940s, scores of young men and women, many on their prom night, were killed in this catastrophic blaze. Local teachers and professors from the surrounding schools and colleges were called on to assist

131

authorities in making death notifications to the victims' families. As the evening and following day progressed, some of the more observant educators began to notice marked behavioral patterns among the grieving families. Such mechanisms as denial and anger were repeated from household to household. From these observations grew discussions that, in turn, grew into theories.

Bard came to recognize these theories' implications for police work and began to work out a strategy for dealing with that growing police problem, that is, family disputes. What Bard proposed was an experiment in one of New York City's most active precincts—the 30th, in west Harlem. Thirty volunteer officers were carefully oriented, trained, and assigned to a special Family Crisis Intervention Unit (FCIU).

The experiment lasted two years, at which time data from both the 30th precinct and an adjoining control precinct were compared. What Bard demonstrated in this comparison was that the experimental precinct had fewer call-backs to the same households for family disputes than the control precinct. This was interpreted as a reduction of violence within the households interacting with FCIU as compared to those in which old methods were used.

The special team of officers had demonstrated that there was another way to handle family disputes. The new method enabled people to calm their immediate crisis and, perhaps, improve their overall home environment. In addition, the likelihood of officer-precipitated violence, unnecessary arrests, and injury was reduced. To an ailing police/court system, FCI was seen as the great hope. Just how did it work?

From research on the behavior of crisis victims, Bard saw that certain techniques were valuable in reducing anger and anxiety, rendering the persons involved more open to reasoning out a solution to their predicament. Therefore, a variety of strategies were used that included *separating* the disputing parties, allowing each to *verbally ventilate* toward the officer, offering *words of encouragement* and of a calming nature, and finally, *mediating*. When each disputant was in a much calmer state, the parties could be brought back together to deal with their problem through any one or more of the following ways: *negotiation, mediation,* and/or *referral* to a helping agency, all accomplished by the officers.

Arrest, as an outcome in the FCI model, was never discounted. However, by almost all concerned officers, police brass, and the courts, it was the outcome of last resort. What must be borne in mind is that this occurred in 1967, the year in which New York State amended its divorce laws so that for the first time in that state, divorce was possible without proving adultery. There were no advocacy groups for victims of domestic violence; the term itself had not yet been created. And so, the nation's largest police department embraced FCI, no longer as an experiment carried out by a small cadre of volunteer officers, but rather as the standard operational procedure for all officers throughout the city. Other departments soon followed. What was better for policing during the turbulent sixties than to embrace a psychologic technique that calmed people down and reduced the likelihood of police use of force?

Domestic Violence

Today FCI remains an important step on the ladder to professional policing for two very important reasons. First, it led to other applications of crisis intervention in police work by Bard and others, specifically, victimology and death notifications. These techniques have helped countless people in times of their most desperate need. Second, FCI techniques are still important in the approach to a domestic violence incident. The abilities to reduce the threat of immediate violence and to quickly gain information from people are essential in all aspects of police work.

However, the main issue for FCI was whether these techniques of mediation and negotiation could survive in the transition from experimental pilot to agency-wide use. A second concern was whether the technique of referral could survive a world that had not yet identified a phenomenon called wife abuse. Finally, there was concern about whether the informal, nonarrest policy could survive a world where women were discovering their rights to due process of law.

Battered Wives by Del Martin (1976) was one of the very first books to deal with what Ralph really meant by "Bang! Zoom! Right to the moon, Alice!" It was a book devoted to disclosing the plight of wives and common law wives within the institution of marriage and common law marriage. The book made many bold and shocking statements about the frequency, level, and range of wife abuse. It demonstrated that wife beating was a common phenomenon, not only in America but around the world, and that such abuse generally increased in severity with time, often requiring hospitalization. Martin suggested that wife beating didn't know any socioeconomic boundaries. And so, as the police and family courts were going about their business of attempting to mediate, negotiate, and refer family members to helping agencies, the very ground they stood on was shifting beneath their feet; unfortunately they barely realized it.

Even if FCI had worked as well in general use as it had in Bard's experimental model, it is doubtful that it would have survived the women's awareness era of the early and mid-1970s. It is, however, a moot point because it didn't work as well as intended, for several reasons. First, Bard spent 30 intense days training and orienting the experimental team of volunteer officers. No agency could replicate that amount of training on a single issue for all its officers. Second, the experimental team was very knowledgeable about the agencies to which they made referrals. Finally, and often overlooked, is the geography of the experiment. Harlem, in the 1960s, despite all its sophistication and uniqueness, was still a predominately black community, policed by a predominately white police force. Both residents and officers were able to endure this predicament by developing a calm, but superficial, dialogue. It was in this medium that the FCI team worked. They were able to successfully make follow-up visits to families to ensure that everything was going well. It is doubtful whether such follow-up visits, often unannounced, could have survived outside the unique relationship of Harlem residents and Harlem cops of the 1960s.

By 1976, the New York City Police Department and the family court's probation department were being sued by a group of woman attorneys headed by Marjory Fields, then of the Brooklyn Legal Services Corp. B., Family Law Unit. The case at hand was *Bruno v. Codd*, and the class action issue was "due process of law" (*Bruno v. Codd* 1977). Mrs. Bruno's contention was that despite numerous visits by the police following beatings by her husband, the police consistently denied her requests to have her husband arrested. She contended that the most the officers would do was to refer her to family court and tell her husband to "calm down and take a walk." After Mrs. Bruno finally did get her husband to family court, and despite his violations of protective orders, the probation department refused her requests to have him arrested for violating court mandated prohibitions. By 1977, the case was before the appellate court, the second rung of three in New York's judicial system, and it was now known as *Bruno v. McGuire*, because McGuire replaced Codd as Police Commissioner. Commissioner McGuire sought to end the case by arbitration. So, in that year, the New York City Police Department signed a consent decree with the plaintiffs. The agency thereby became the first major police department in the United States to have an affirmative arrest policy for domestic violence cases.

It is more than interesting to note that the probation department eventually fought off the *Bruno* challenge in the state's highest court. The implication was that the New York City Police Department became the only law enforcement entity in the state to have an affirmative arrest policy for husband/wife violence cases. It meant that the nation's largest police department was out of synchronization. Had the department where FCI originated, now the prescribed methodology of nearly all police departments in the country, become the victim of legal meddling by women's advocates? This certainly was the view of many officers at all levels within the department itself. This situation made it more interesting to see how policies and practices began to evolve.

I have referred to the *Bruno* agreement as an "affirmative arrest policy." This term is one of my own choosing. I have adopted it over time to draw a distinction between it and a "mandatory arrest policy." The differences may seem subtle and trivial, but they have strikingly different outcomes in terms of franchising or disfranchising the victims of domestic violence. I shall elaborate on this at the conclusion of this chapter. For now, it is only necessary to know the differences between "affirmative" and "mandatory" arrest policies.

First, *an affirmative policy may have components that are mandatory, whereas a mandatory policy is mandatory throughout.* For example, in the New York City Police Department's policy, the result of *Bruno* provides that in all cases in which a felony is committed, or where the criminal terms of an order of protection are violated, the officer must make an arrest. That is the "mandatory" element to the arrest policy. Where the officer had reasonable cause to believe that a misdemeanor (the majority of cases) had been committed, he or she shall not decline to make an arrest if the aggrieved party so wishes. This leaves to the victim, in the vast majority of cases, the power to initiate a legal action. A mandatory policy would extend the "must arrest" prescription to all cases, therefore effectively removing any vestiges of power from the victim. Some jurisdictions, either through individual department policy or through legislation, as in the case of the state of Washington, have adopted mandatory arrest policies.

Which of the two, affirmative or mandatory, is more effective in reducing domestic violence is at the center of a controversial debate in today's law enforcement community. Supporters of mandatory arrest policies lean heavily on several recent domestic violence studies. The most often cited is the Minneapolis Study. This experiment had officers apply one of three random outcomes to domestic violence misdemeanor assault cases. One outcome was arrest. Another was mediation and referral. The third was the "take a walk and cool down" strategy. The experiment showed that arrest halved the recidivism of the "take a walk" strategy (26 percent to 13 percent), while mediation fell somewhere in the middle (18 percent).

There are many critics and supporters of the study (U.S. Department of Justice 1984). The most vocal supporters are often members of domestic violence advocacy groups, which are often indistinguishable from women's rights groups. The critics tend to be largely from the law enforcement community, for the most part, departments that have embraced FCI as their agency's approach to the problem. However, one critic is Dr. Richard Gelles, of the University of Rhode Island, who has written over a half dozen books on domestic violence. He is skeptical of these recent studies. He cites poor research design, inadequate samples, and difficulties with randomness as major problems. Further, he expresses concern that many law enforcement agencies are implementing mandatory arrest policies as a result of these studies. Gelles himself sees a family nurturing model similar to FCI as the future direction for domestic violence problems.

Affirmative Arrest—Empowering Victims

For the past decade, the movement toward mandatory arrest by domestic violence advocacy groups has created an equal and opposite tug by many within law enforcement. These chiefs and sheriffs support FCI as the professional police model. Often overlooked in the debate is the affirmative arrest policy, where both FCI and mandatory arrest elements come together to provide victims with both confidence and protection.

Consider for a moment the mandatory elements of New York City's affirmative arrest policy. In the felony situation, an arrest must be made when the officer has reasonable cause to believe a felony has been committed. A felony in New York State, as in most jurisdictions, is punishable by a year or more in prison. It is regarded as a serious offense and, in terms of violence, involves either the infliction of serious physical injury, or injury by use of a weapon. Certainly, it is in the compelling interest of the people of a state to demonstrate their intolerance to this level of violence, even if an individual victim cannot, or wishes not to, press charges. On the issue of orders of protection, officers must make an arrest if any criminal conduct, prohibited within the context of the orders of protection, is committed. Here again, the state shows a compelling interest to review the conduct of matters previously brought before the court. The victims in these cases have sought the protection of the court and have summoned the police for assistance. To use the order of protection without judicial review invites possible abuse of the order's power and authority.

However, even under the mandatory aspects of an affirmative arrest policy, the married domestic violence victim in New York State is still entitled to exercise a great deal of power by the right to choose either family court (a civil action) or criminal court. This is applicable for both felonies and misdemeanors in the vast majority of offenses committed within household settings. These include, in New York State, second- and third-degree assault, first- and second-degree reckless endangerment, menacing, disorderly conduct, and harassment.

But how can the victim, frightened, humiliated, angered, and perhaps seriously injured, render a good judgment under such conditions? Obviously, not without a fair degree of help. This brings us back to FCI. Bard's work and the work of others have demonstrated that police officers, in their approach to victims, can make an immediate and lasting difference, positive or negative, in victims' ability to deal with their individual dilemma. Intervention techniques such as allowing ventilation, giving support, asking the victim's permission or preference, allowing the victim to make decisions toward his or her future, and assuring the victim that certain decisions were good decisions go a long way in helping people cope with their crises.

So, too, has the situation changed in terms of referrals; not referrals as a substitute for a denied arrest but referrals as a resource for both victims who choose a legal remedy and those who don't. Today, victim advocacy groups, women's shelters, and batterers' treatment programs are a far cry from what was available only a decade ago. Even the legal threshold for divorce has changed more in the last 20 years than in the preceding 200 years.

Police practices are also far more accurately measurable in a department with an affirmative arrest policy. Police practice can differ radically from official police policy. Although most police agencies still need to implement better methods for recording and tracking domestic violence cases, an affirmative arrest policy, as opposed to FCI, is a giant step for monitoring and evaluating police performance in handling domestic violence. In a system nearly devoid of an arrest outcome, the need for counting is diminished. This lessens the need to monitor, which in turn leads to the type of conditions that brought about a *Bruno* case.

Discussion

There certainly is a need for more in-depth research, directed more toward the prevention and treatment of domestic violence than at immediate police action. Furthermore, there is a certain expectation that the public has regarding the emergency aspect of police work.

Calling the police is much like calling an ambulance. No one really likes to call an ambulance, but under certain conditions he or she sees no other alternative. Even after the ambulance arrives, the caller often hopes that the ambulance attendant can solve the problem and that a trip to the hospital will not be necessary. However, once the patient is removed, the patient and family shift their focus to the hospital, its doctors, and staff. Here the concern is, how good is the care and how effective is the treatment? Although research can improve an emergency medical response, we don't devote 90 percent of our medical research to ambulance protocol.

Unfortunately, research beyond police response in domestic violence is slow to catch on. Once it does, it will be a boon for prosecutors, judges, probation agents, and service providers. However, most important is the need for educational research and using the results toward education in the prevention of domestic violence.

The Minneapolis Study, aside from revealing recidivism rates as they compared to police treatment, also revealed that 45 percent of the households responded to lacked a marriage relationship. This fact gave New York City additional incentive to expand its "affirmative arrest policy" beyond the husband–wife context of the *Bruno* consent decree. A joint project currently underway, involving the New York City Police Department and the Victim Services Agency, is aimed at a dual police/service provider approach to troubled households. Before program success could even be evaluated, the project began to drive the participants toward developing a new method of discerning which cases, among a myriad of police calls, were actually incidents of domestic violence. The methodology to identify and track cases, in turn, became an important tool of the department itself in evaluating police performance agency-wide. Such spin-off from police research is essential to fine tuning future police policy. Therefore, research should always be in motion, open to both observation and criticism.

Conclusion

Police policy and practice must remain aligned. They cannot deviate from basic principles of justice and human well-being. No policy or practice, for the sake of expediency or economy, can violate these basic principles. Nor can extreme views on criminal justice research or civil rights be allowed to trample the well-being of victims or the rights of defendants. For now, it seems that the "affirmative arrest policy" approach to domestic violence is the best course to steer. However, the real test for us, as a society, is to strengthen our interpersonal relationships, particularly our family/household relationships. When we accomplish this, we will not only win a great criminal justice victory, but also will raise ourselves as a society and as a species.

References

Bard M: Training the Police as Specialists in Family Crisis Intervention. Washington DC, National Institute of Law Enforcement and Criminal Justice, 1970

Bruno v. Codd, 90 Misc. 2nd 1047, 396 N.Y.S. 2nd 974, 976 (Sup. Ct. N.Y. Co. 1977)

Martin D: Battered Wives. San Francisco, Glide Publications, 1976

Sherman L, Berk R: Police Responses to Domestic Assault: Preliminary Findings. Washington, DC, Police Foundation, 1983

U.S. Department of Justice, Attorney General: Attorney General's Task Force on Family Violence. Washington, DC, U.S. Department of Justice, 1984

Chapter 8

Enforcing the Law Against Wife Abusers: The Role of Mental Health Professionals

LISA G. LERMAN, J.D., LL.M.

Chapter 8

Enforcing the Law Against Wife Abusers: The Role of Mental Health Professionals

Responses to wife abuse, or battering, by the institutions from which abused women seek help may be divided into two categories, based on the fundamental differences in the objectives of the response. One category of response may be characterized as *conciliation*, in which the parties are referred to mediation or therapy outside of the legal system and in which the violence is treated as evidence of a relational problem rather than as a crime. This type of response often includes an attempt to repair and preserve the relationship of the abuser and the victim. The other category, which may be characterized as *law enforcement*, includes responses that focus on formal legal action designed to punish or rehabilitate the perpetrator and to protect the victim from further acts of violence.

Psychiatrists and other mental health professionals have a role to play in either case, because the law enforcement system inevitably seeks the help of mental health institutions, either to get rid of the cases or to ensure that they are handled more effectively or both. Psychiatrists who have patients who are abusers or victims of abuse may respond to the violence in ways that help to stop the violence or help to perpetuate it. Whether the patients are court referred or not, the response of mental health professionals may be characterized as a law enforcement type of response or as a conciliation type of response. If the incidence of battering in our society is to be reduced, it is necessary that all professionals who encounter people who are in battering relationships address the violence as a type of behavior that is against the law and cannot be tolerated. This means holding the perpetrator of the violence, *not* the victim, responsible for the violence, and helping the victim to understand and assert her right not to be battered.

What follows is an explanation of why a law enforcement response is necessary to stop battering, a few examples of how conciliation responses may help to perpetuate violence, and some thoughts about the implications of this analysis for mental health professionals.

The Need for Law Enforcement

The Epidemic of Battering

In order to describe the responses to battering that are needed, it is necessary to briefly describe the nature and scope of the problem. Ganley (1981) describes four types of battering: 1) physical battering, including all aggressive acts done to the body of another; 2) sexual violence, including physical attacks on the sex organs of another or forced sexual activity; 3) psychological battering, which includes all forms of emotional abuse by a person who has committed at least one act of physical battering; and 4) destruction of property or pets, which may be done for the purpose of controlling or threatening another person. Battering occurs in all racial, economic, and religious groups, and in rural, urban, and suburban settings (Straus et al. 1980). Battering occurs in marital, pre-marital, and post-marital relationships (Stark et al. 1981). The overwhelming majority of the perpetrators are male and the victims are female (Dobash and Dobash 1979).

Adequate data on the incidence of battering have not yet been compiled, but the existing data provide a glimpse of the massive numbers of people affected. Reports from the FBI indicate that one-third of female homicide victims in the United States are killed by their husbands or boyfriends (U.S.

Department of Justice, FBI 1984; U.S. Department of Justice, Attorney General 1984). A Harris poll done in Kentucky reported that 1 in 10 of the over 2,000 women interviewed reported having experienced some violence from her husband during the 12 months that preceded the interview (Shulman 1979). A Connecticut study showed that about half of the injuries of women treated at an emergency room resulted from battering (Stark et al. 1981). Nationally it is estimated that one-third of police time is spent responding to domestic violence calls (O'Reilley 1983).

Institutional Perpetuation of Violence

What one perceives to be the causes of battering will determine what one perceives to be the appropriate response. There are many different explanations of violence that implicate the psychologic makeup of the parties. It has been asserted by some that victims of abuse are masochistic (for example, Snell et al. 1964) and by others that victims are unable, because of the ways that women are socialized, to assert themselves to stop the violence (Walker 1979). Some writers have argued that men learn to use violence to solve problems and have difficulty in identifying or expressing feelings other than anger or aggression (for example, Ganley 1981). Most people have discarded the idea that the violence is caused by the masochism of the victims, but the other psychologic theories appear to be quite useful in working with individuals. However, battering has reached such an epidemic level that one must begin to examine both the underlying social causes of violence, as does Lystad (1985), and the institutional responses that fail to stop, that accept, or that even perpetuate intimate violence.

Traditionally, husbands were legally responsible for their wives and children, and were permitted to use force to punish misconduct (Civil Rights Commission 1982). It was not until the second half of the 19th century that most states prohibited physical assaults on spouses. Until the 1970s, however, there

147

was little effort to enforce this prohibition, and victims were virtually without recourse. Police refused to make arrests or file reports on assaults that were committed by men against their wives or girlfriends (Parnas 1967). Prosecutors refused to file charges, and judges refused to penalize the abusers or protect the victims (Field and Field 1973). Within the last 10 years, law enforcement agencies have begun to make some changes, but progress is slow.

Other institutions from which abused women seek help have been similarly apathetic in their responses to battering. Many mental health professionals have tended to blame the victims for the violence, have claimed that the victims provoked their mates, and have asserted that the solution lies in behavioral change by the victims. Some doctors have regarded abused women as hysterics and prescribed tranquilizers to relieve the psychologic symptoms of battering. This "treatment" may solve some problems but may create others, because a victim of abuse who is sedated may be less able to protect herself or to escape a violent situation than she would be without medication (Stark et al. 1982).

The church has also been guilty of acting in a way that perpetuates the violence by blaming the victims and defining marriage to include a wifely duty of obedience. A few years ago I appeared on the "700 Club" to talk about spousal rape and was horrified to hear the show's host ask his six million housewife viewers to get down on their knees in front of their television sets and pray that they would be more obedient wives so that their husbands would not abuse them any longer.

In order to reduce the incidence of battering it is necessary to change the responses of all professionals and institutions to whom people in battering relationships go for help. Too often the general response of institutions has been that battering is a private matter, that it is at least partly the fault of the victim, and that there is very little that anyone can do to help.

Law Enforcement as a Deterrent

The purpose of the criminal justice system is to communicate to the community the types of behavior that are so damaging to society that they are not to be tolerated. The state pays police, prosecutors, and judges to enforce criminal laws so that the prohibitions stated in the criminal laws will be taken seriously. The best responses to domestic violence are those that assist the criminal justice system in the effective communication of the message that violence is prohibited and that those who commit acts of violence will suffer the consequences.

There is much disagreement as to the possibility of real deterrence, but a recent study of police responses to battering appears to indicate that many abusers can be deterred through law enforcement. This study, conducted in Minneapolis by the Police Foundation (Sherman and Berk 1983), tested the efficacy of three different police responses: arrest, separation of the parties, and mediation in deterring subsequent assault. The police were divided into three groups, which responded differently to comparable domestic violence calls. One group made arrests, one group separated the parties for eight hours, and one group conducted informal mediation. A six-month follow-up survey revealed that there had been a recurrence of violence in 24 percent of the cases in which police had separated the parties, a 17 percent recurrence in cases which were mediated, and only a 10 percent recurrence of violence in cases in which an arrest was made. The sociologists found the data on arrest and separation to be a statistically significant indication that *law enforcement deters violence.*

Many of the men who are batterers have little experience with the criminal justice system and have an investment in avoiding being convicted of crimes. A good example of such a person is John Fedders, former Chief of Enforcement at the Securities and Exchange Commission, who resigned during a great deal of publicity about his history of wife abuse.

I worked with a program in Miami that accepted for counseling abusers who had been arrested and jailed the night before they were referred to the program. Several observed interviews of these men were very revealing. These interviews took place in jail at 6:45 A.M. Most had never been arrested before; one was an international banker in a three-piece suit. These men were deeply affected by having spent the night in jail and were asking many questions about their own behavior. Those who seemed unaffected were those who had criminal records, for whom this was not a new experience. For them, perhaps longer term incarceration may be the only effective way to stop the violence. For the others, however, a cooperative working relationship between law enforcement and mental health agencies may offer both the power to compel changes in conduct and the assistance that abusers need to learn to stop the violence.

The Role of Mental Health Professionals

Psychiatrists and other mental health professionals, like everyone else who encounters people in abusive relationships, may respond in ways that either condemn or tacitly accept the occurrence of battering. Some questions that are raised by recent developments in the law enforcement response to battering include the following: First, whether the professional knows about the violence that is perpetrated by or against his or her patients and whether the mental health professional seeks out information when there is some indication that there has been violence or treats the issue as a personal or private matter or even as irrelevant. Second, when the violence is discovered, does the professional understand the barriers imposed by the frequent desire of both victims and abusers to deny the existence of a problem? One Washington, D.C., police officer, who works as a counselor in a program for men who batter, says that he assumes that the seriousness of the violence is three times whatever he is told.

Third, is the therapist familiar with the legal remedies and the programs that exist in the community to assist people in violent relationships, so that what the law requires or permits can be explained, or appropriate referrals can be made? If the mental health professional is the only or the primary person to whom a victim or an abuser goes for help, then his or her response to the issue of violence may be the only information that the patient gets about his or her rights or responsibilities.

In discussing violence with an abuser, for example, it may be useful to provide him with some information about what types of behavior are and are not crimes and what the maximum penalties are that may be imposed. If an abuser attempts to justify violence by explaining that his wife was verbally abusive, it might be appropriate to point out that most verbal nastiness is not against the law, but that beating someone up is a crime.

In discussing violence with a victim of abuse, it may be useful for the professional to provide information about what remedies are provided by law and what sources of assistance are available in the community. Mental health professionals are not permitted to give legal advice, but can explain in general what is available under the civil protection order law in their state and what types of conduct could be prosecuted as crimes. Just knowing what the law says may affect the victim's perception of her options and may help her to stop believing that the violence is her fault.

A fourth question is, What assumptions does the mental health professional have about battering relationships, and how do they affect his or her response to issues of violence? It is important that all mental health professionals be aware of their own attitudes, that is, whether they tend to identify with male patients in troubled relationships and excuse or overlook criminal violence or whether they tend to think that women who really didn't want to get hit would leave their mates. Such assumptions may result in responses that may help to perpetuate patterns of violence.

Finally, does the professional tend to encourage people who have violent marital problems to try to preserve their marriages? For many victims of abuse, leaving their relationships with their abusers may be appropriate and necessary. Not doing so may mean accepting a continuing risk of injury or death. In dealing with violent relationships, a presumption in favor of reconciliation may be very dangerous.

Mental health professionals must understand their responsibility to respond to reports of battering with the goal of stopping the violence. If the mental health worker defines his or her professional role in a way that makes this an inappropriate goal, then he or she may in fact be part of an institutional response that, by failing to insist that the violence must stop, allows it to continue.

References

Civil Rights Commission: Under the Rule of Thumb: Battered Women and the Administration of Justice. Washington, DC, Civil Rights Commission, 1982

Dobash RE, Dobash R: Violence Against Wives: A Case Against the Patriarchy. New York, Free Press, 1979

Field M, Field H: Marital violence and the criminal process: neither justice nor peace. Social Service Review 47:221, 1973

Ganley A: Court-Mandated Counseling for Men Who Batter: A Three-Day Workshop for Mental Health Professionals. Washington, DC, Center for Women Policy Studies, 1981

Lystad M: Prevention of Family Violence. Proceedings of the American Psychiatric Association, 1986

Parnas R: The Police Response to the Domestic Disturbance. Wisconsin Law Review 914, 1967

O'Reilley J: Wife-beating: the silent crime. Time Magazine, September 5, 1983, p. 23

Sherman L, Berk R: Police Responses to Domestic Assault: Preliminary Findings. Washington, DC, Police Foundation, 1983

Shulman M: A Survey of Spousal Violence Against Women in Kentucky. Washington, DC, U.S. Government Printing Office, 1979

Snell J, Rosenwald R, Robey A: The wifebeater's wife: a study of family interaction. Arch Gen Psychiatry 11:107, 1964

Stark E, Flitcraft A, Zuckerman D, et al: Wife Abuse in the Medical Setting: An Introduction for Health Personnel. Rockville, MD, National Clearinghouse on Domestic Violence, 1981

Straus M, Gelles R, Steinmetz S, et al: Behind Closed Doors: Violence in the American Family. New York, Doubleday, 1980

U.S. Department of Justice, Attorney General: Attorney General's Task Force on Family Violence. Washington, DC, 1984

U.S. Department of Justice, FBI: Uniform Crime Reports for 1983. Washington, DC, U.S. Government Printing Office, 1984

Walker L: The Battered Woman. New York, Harper and Row, 1979

Chapter 9

Intervention Programs for Individual Victims and Their Families

CAROL C. NADELSON, M.D.
MARIA SAUZIER, M.D.

Chapter 9

Intervention Programs for Individual Victims and Their Families

Spouse Abuse

Violence has been estimated to occur in 50 percent of American families (Gelles 1974; Straus 1977–78). Although generally concerns about family violence focus on child abuse, more recently spouse abuse has been identified as a substantial problem. Spouse abuse is not limited to a particular social class or ethnic group. Although the highest reported incidence is among the poor, this is probably because they are more likely to come to the attention of public agencies and legal authorities. A study of 600 couples who were in the process of divorce bears this out: 40 percent of lower class women and 23 percent of middle-class women reported physical abuse by spouses (Levinger 1966). Stark et al. (1979) emphasized that physicians vastly underestimated the amount of battering in the patient population; thus, while Rounsaville and Weissman (1977–78) reported that 3.8 percent of the women presenting to an emergency trauma service and 3.4 percent of the women presenting to an emergency psychiatric service had been battered by men with whom they were intimate, Stark et al. put the figure from the same services reported by Rounsaville and Weissman at 25 percent. Other authors (Hilberman and Munson 1977–78;

157

Rosenfeld 1979) confirm the tendency toward underreporting.

Of all the murders in this country, 20 to 50 percent occur within the family. One study reported that 40 percent of the homicides in a major U.S. city were between spouses (Kansas City Police Department 1973), and the Federal Bureau of Investigation estimates that one out of every four women who is murdered is killed by her husband or boyfriend (Federal Bureau of Investigation 1982).

Wife beating is often accompanied by physical and/or sexual abuse of the children (Gayford 1975; Hilberman and Munson 1977–78; Scott 1974), and children who are abused often grow up to abuse their offspring. In addition, children who see violent interactions often have physically abusive relationships in adulthood.

Clinicians have been impressed with the frequency with which child abuse and spouse abuse occur together. Gayford (1975) reported that 37 percent of the women and 54 percent of the men who had been abused beat their children; Hilberman and Munson (1977–78) identified physical and/or sexual abuse of children in a third of the families they studied. Emotional neglect, abuse, alcoholism, and frequent separations were the norms, and children in violent homes were witnesses and targets of abuse (Gayford 1975; Gelles 1974; Hilberman and Munson 1977–78; Scott 1974; Walker 1979).

Thus, lifelong violence begins with early and repeated patterns in childhood for both men and women who are later involved in abuse (Gayford 1975; Gelles 1974; Hilberman and Munson 1977–78; Pizzey 1974; Rounsaville 1978; Scott 1974; Walker 1979). Suicides and homicides among family members and neighborhood acquaintances occur frequently. Studies indicate that most of the women left home at an early age to escape from violent and seductive fathers. They tended to marry while teenagers and many were pregnant at the time of marriage or had had children before marriage. They viewed pregnancy as the only way they would be allowed to leave the family. Further, most women reported an increase in the pattern of violence during pregnancy (Hilberman and Munson 1977–78), often leading to abortions and premature births (Gayford 1975; Gelles 1974; Hilberman and Munson 1977–78; Walker 1979).

In these families, violence often erupted when a husband felt that his needs were not gratified or when he was drunk. Frequently, this occurred after he had been with another woman. The assaults usually happened at night and on weekends, so children were witnesses and participants when they attempted to defend or protect the mother. An association between alcohol use and marital violence has been noted (Gayford 1975; Gelles 1974; Hilberman and Munson 1977–78). Drinking accompanied by violence occurred in 22 to 100 percent of those reported, and many spouse abusers who were alcoholics were also abusers when they were sober.

In looking at the predictors of future violence, Walker (1984) notes,

> The best prediction of future violence was a history of past violent behavior. This included witnessing, receiving, and committing violent acts in their childhood home; violent acts toward pets, inanimate objects, or other people; previous criminal records; longer time in the military; and previous expression of violent behavior toward women. If these items are added to a history of temper tantrums, insecurity, need to keep the environment stable, easily threatened by minor upsets, jealousy, possessiveness, and the ability to be charming, manipulative, and seductive to get what he wants, and hostile, nasty, and mean when he doesn't succeed—then the risk for battering becomes very high. If alcohol abuse problems are included, the pattern becomes classic. (pp. 10–11)

Walker (1984) indicates that a certain combination of factors seems to suggest higher risk potential. One, which is also mentioned by Straus et al. (1981), is the difference in sociodemographic variables between the batterers and the battered women. Batterers tend to be less educated than their wives and from lower socioeconomic classes as well as different ethnic, religious, or racial groups. Men who are more traditional than women in their attitudes toward women's roles are potentially at higher risk; these men measure a woman's feelings for them by how well she meets the sex-role expectations they have defined.

These men are also in need of a great amount of nurturance and are very possessive of women's time (Hilberman and Munson 1977–78; Martin 1976). Extreme jealousy was reported in a large percentage of these marriages (Gayford 1975; Gelles 1974; Hilberman and Munson 1977–78; Scott 1974). Husbands made active efforts to keep their wives isolated. If the women left the house for any reason, they were often accused of infidelity and were assaulted. Friendships with women were discouraged, and husbands often embarrassed their wives in the presence of their friends by asserting that they were lesbians, prostitutes, or otherwise unacceptable.

The women often felt sorry for their husbands because of their histories of deprivation and abuse. Many women left their marriages for brief periods but returned because of economic and emotional dependence on husbands and threats of further violence from which they had no protection (Hilberman and Munson 1977–78; Scott 1974). Some women were assaulted daily, while others were beaten intermittently and lived in constant anticipatory terror (Dewsbury 1975; Fonseka 1974; Gayford 1975; Gelles 1974; Hilberman and Munson 1977–78; Martin 1976; Scott 1974; Walker 1979). Guns were available in most of these homes and were constant threats (Hilberman and Munson 1977–78).

Some women sought recourse through the criminal justice system, but these attempts were often frustrated by the unresponsiveness of officials, as well as by threats of retaliation by the husband (Chapman and Gates 1978; Eisenberg and Micklow 1976; Field and Field 1973; Gates 1977; Hilberman and Munson 1977–78; Walker 1979). While most women were passive and did not defend themselves, the few women who themselves resorted to violence did so in desperation when other options had failed. They used violence in response to direct threats to their lives, and their behavior usually surprised them. They were often unaware of the extent of their rage and their capacity for violence (Hilberman and Munson 1977–78).

Impact of Abuse

Hilberman and Munson (1977–78) have described a response pattern among the battered women that is similar to that described for the rape–trauma syndrome. Terror was constant but since chronicity and unpredictability were also characteristic, severe agitation and anxiety with fears of imminent doom were also present (Burgess and Holmstrom 1974a). These women were unable to relax or sleep, and at night they experienced violent nightmares. During the daytime they were passive and lacked energy. They experienced a pervasive sense of hopelessness and despair. They often saw themselves as deserving abuse and as powerless to change their lives.

Frequently, there were somatic symptoms reported such as headaches, asthma, gastrointestinal symptoms, and chronic pain. More than half of these women had prior psychiatric histories. Depression was the most frequent diagnosis. They had often sought medical help and many had been treated for drug overdoses and suicide attempts. Although they had multiple medical contacts over many years, they did not tell their physicians of the abuse, nor were they asked (Dewsbury 1975; Hilberman and Munson 1977–78).

A high incidence of somatic, psychologic, and behavioral dysfunctions have also been described in their children. These included headaches, abdominal complaints, asthma, and peptic ulcer. Depression, suicidal behavior, and psychosis were also reported (Gayford 1975; Hilberman and Munson 1977–78). For the preschool and young schoolchildren, somatic complaints, stuttering, school phobias, enuresis, and insomnia were frequent. Insomnia was often accompanied by intense fear, screaming, and resistance to going to bed at night. Most children had impaired concentration and difficulty with schoolwork. Among older children, aggressive disruptive behavior, stealing, temper tantrums, truancy, and fighting with siblings and schoolmates were characteristics of boys, whereas girls were more likely to experience somatic symptoms.

Counseling Implications

The response to family violence is often blame and disbelief. This is supported by the tendency of victims to deny the problem and by their difficulty in acknowledging anger about it. This occurs, in part, because they fear losing control, especially because of their close relationship with the abuser. As a result, aggression may be directed against themselves or those who try to help.

Several studies provide evidence of the profoundly self-destructive behaviors that emerge after victimization. In comparing 59 abused and neglected children with 29 neglected children and 30 children who were neither abused nor neglected, Green (1978) found self-destructive behaviors exhibited by 40.6 percent of the abused, 17.2 percent of the neglected, and 6.7 percent of the controls. He concluded, "the abused child's sense of worthlessness, badness and self-hatred as a consequence of parental assault, rejection and scapegoating form the nucleus for self-destructive behavior" (p. 581).

Fear, especially in the presence of continuing threats, appears to be a major deterrent to activity (Martin 1976; Symonds 1978). Another reason for the reluctance to leave may be "learned helplessness," the inability to effect change, which has been described by many authors as a particular problem for women (Ball and Wyman 1977–78; Seligman 1975; Waites 1977–78; Walker 1977–78, 1984). Certainly, the reaction of hostages, the "Stockholm syndrome," where positive feelings, perhaps based on terror, dependence, and gratitude, is seen also in battered women. Further, some women experience what has been called "learned hopeful-ness," which leads them to think, "I hope he will change and get better" or "I hope I can change him." This may be a possible explanation for the behavior of battered women (Ochberg 1980). These issues must be understood by those working with family violence.

Counselors working with these women often become frustrated and angry at their passivity, failure to follow through on suggestions, and the frequency with which they return to the abusive situation (Federal Bureau of Investiga-tion 1972, 1974; Hilberman and Munson 1977–78; Walker 1977–78, 1979). Attempts to rescue victims and overidentifi-cation with the helplessness and dependency may support and reinforce abusive behavior and prevent these women from acting on their own behalf (Ball and Wyman 1977–78; Ridington 1977–78).

Women are often reluctant to reveal the extent of their problem because of their mistrust and low self-esteem. It is difficult for them to establish trusting relationships, even with those who promise help, since they expect deception and they have no basis for trust. Further, they are often unaware of the rage they harbor because of long-standing suppression of these feelings, and as indicated above, fear of loss of control may become a predominant theme and increase the difficulty of achieving autonomy.

While involvement of the abuser in counseling may be an important therapeutic goal, it may also be counterproduc-tive in some cases, until individual psychotherapy has enabled the abused to establish some control and autonomy (Straus 1974; Pizzey 1975). In addition, interventions must be directed at the reality of the victim's life circumstances to provide necessary medical care, legal counseling, and social supports. Services must be coordinated and the victim supported and educated.

Counseling usually involves a short-term issue-oriented crisis approach, with the goal of restoring the victim to her previous level of functioning as quickly as possible (Burgess and Holmstrom 1974b). Attention must also be paid to the possibility of long-term symptoms such as those seen in post-traumatic stress disorders. Symptoms such as those described above may be delayed in onset for months to years after the abusive situation has changed. At times, events later in life will trigger earlier traumatic experiences and foster symptom development. Walker (1984) has emphasized that these women are more successful at reversing helplessness when they leave the relationship than when they remain. Further, a Washington, D.C., Police Foundation study (1983) revealed that the most effective deterrent to repeated incidents of violence of men against wives or girlfriends is arrest.

A Model Program for Sexually Abused Children and Their Families

The prevalence of sexual abuse of children in our culture is now well documented. As early as 1953, Kinsey gathered data about all aspects of human sexuality and revealed that 23 percent of women had had abusive sexual experiences in their childhoods. The prevalence of father–daughter incest, which represents only one kind of sexual abuse, is estimated to be one percent, on a par with schizophrenia and diabetes (Herman and Hirschman 1981a).

In Massachusetts, there has been a major and steady increase of incidents reported to the Department of Social Services each year: 1,400 cases in 1981; 2,142 in 1982; 2,938 in 1983; and 5,325 in 1984 (Department of Social Services 1981–84). This increase is seen by most experts as representing a greater likelihood of revelation and report, rather than an increase in actual occurrence.

There are several prerequisites to reporting sexual abuse: an awareness of sexual abuse as a problem, knowledge about available resources, and trust that reporting will be beneficial. Public education has affected awareness and knowledge, but the benefits of revelation and reporting are often questioned by media accounts of inappropriate interventions. Among clinicians there is still no consensus about the effectiveness of reporting sexual abuse of a child. The absence of an established and tested intervention protocol, the paucity of clinicians trained in this field, and the uneven quality of child welfare services offered by different states all combine to lower the incidence of reported sexual abuse.

At this time, it must be acknowledged that all varieties of interventions that are offered to sexually abused children and their families are experimental in the sense that none have been validated by long-term follow-up research. Eighteen-month follow-up data available from one major study reported here (Gomes-Schwartz et al. 1984) have enabled us to develop the model intervention program that is described in this chapter.

Background Data

Information about sexual abuse comes from case histories (Gutheil and Avery 1977; Katan 1973), small-scale psychologic studies (Herman and Hirschman 1981b; Tsai et al. 1979), or large-scale sociologic studies (Finkelhor 1979; Kinsey 1953).

One broad psychologic research project has recently been conducted at New England Medical Center, using 181 cases of sexual abuse (156 confirmed, 25 unconfirmed) (Gomes-Schwartz et al. 1984). Concomitant with data collection was the provision of therapy for the child and his or her family, including the offender.

The children seen were between six months and 18 years old. Seventy-two percent were girls, 28 percent were boys; 29 percent were under six years of age, 37 percent were latency age (7 to 12), and 35 percent were adolescents (13 to 18) at the time of revelation of the abuse. The sexual abuse reported ranged from witnessing an exhibitionist to experiencing sexual intercourse, with some genital contact occurring in 88 percent of the cases. Ninety-four percent of the offenders were male, ranging from teenage babysitters to grandfathers. Their average age was 29. Only 3 percent of offenders were total strangers. Incest in the biological sense occurred in 41 percent of the cases seen. Incest, in the broader current definition, which includes parental figures such as live-in boyfriends, occurred in 62 percent of the cases. Only 21 percent of the abuse occurred as one single incident, either rape or incest. In most cases, incidents occurred over a period of time, some spanning more than five years, with a frequency varying between several times for the whole span of years to more than once a week. Most abuse incidents occurred in places familiar to the child, like his or her home or the perpetrator's home. The families studied were representative of the greater Boston population in terms of race, religion, and socioeconomic status. The only remarkable demographic difference found was a preponderance of single-parent households.

Emotional stress and psychopathology in the children seen were significantly greater than that found in a matched normal population, but less than that found in a matched psychiatric clinic population. Specific symptoms seen varied according to age. Preschool-age children showed age-inappropriate sexual activity and immaturity in their intellectual and prosocial development (for example, acquiring socially valued behaviors, such as discerning between right and wrong). They also showed reactive symptoms such as anxiety, fears, and depression. School-age children also showed age-inappropriate sexual behavior, but less intellectual and social immaturity, and no prosocial deficit. Their presentation was marked by increased aggression, antisocial activity, and fears. As a group, the school-age children showed more emotional disturbance than preschool-age children. Adolescents showed fears of being harmed, anxiety, depression, dependent–inhibited behavior, and hostility. Teenagers who had already run away from home were hospitalized or in youth detention centers, and were not brought to this outpatient clinic. The study thus lacks information about the group of adolescents showing the most serious psychopathology related to sexual abuse experiences.

Research data relevant to the design of a treatment program include correlations between distress levels and various factors related to the abuse. Emotional distress and behavioral problems were related to the degree of violence associated with the abuse more than to any other characteristic of the sexual abuse (for example, type of sexual acts performed, duration). This is consistent with the findings in the rape literature (Burgess and Holmstrom 1974a, 1974b); the sexual assault is primarily an expression of aggression and a quest for power and only secondarily a sexual act.

Incest in the broader sense, perpetrated by nonbiologic father figures (for example, stepfathers, boyfriends of mothers), was related to poorer self-esteem and more behavioral problems than incest performed by biologic fathers or other relatives. There was no difference in the degree of violence, but a significant difference in the way mothers reacted: They were, as a group, more likely to side with a boyfriend or stepfather/husband than with a husband who was the biologic father of the victim. A negative (hostile, blaming, and rejecting) reaction on the part of the victim's mother to the revelation of abuse correlated with the level of emotional distress, low self-esteem, and the symptoms seen. A positive reaction (caring, protecting, and nonblaming) cannot mitigate the effects of abuse, but at least it does not compound them.

Forty-one percent of the mothers of sexual abuse and incest victims had been sexually abused in their own childhoods; 34 percent had been physically abused or neglected. Clinically, they presented a wide spectrum of diagnoses, which did not correlate with their reaction to the revelation of abuse. No significant differences between incest and nonincest mothers were found.

At the 18-month follow-up, most victims showed a significant decrease in psychopathology and an increase in self-esteem. Exceptions were those children who had exhibited few or no symptoms during crisis intervention, but were symptomatic 18 months later. Revictimization was rare (only five percent) in this sample.

Seventy-eight percent of the victims required more than crisis intervention. Those children who received prolonged treatment in a specialized program showed the highest rate of improvement.

These data were gathered between 1980 and 1983, supported by a grant from the Office of Juvenile Justice and Delinquency Prevention, which mandated the provision of therapy concomitant with data collection. A specific model program—the Family Crisis Program (FCP) for Sexually Abused Children—was designed, responding to both the mandate of the grant and the need of the greater Boston community. When grant funding ended in 1984, the need for a specialized sexual abuse program was evident and the program continued on a fee-for-service basis.

Literature Review

Designing a clinical sexual abuse program requires the adaptation of traditional child psychiatric treatment strategies to the special needs of sexually abused children and their families. There is little conclusive information about effective treatment strategies for these families to draw upon (Mrazek and Kempe 1981). A review of the literature on incest reveals that a wide variety of treatment approaches has been advocated. Individual therapy sessions for the child are an essential component of many programs (Burgess et al. 1978). Those who view sexual abuse as a sign of pathology in the family system advocate traditional family therapy (Eist and Mandel 1966). Some therapists have focused almost exclusively on father–daughter incest. For example, Browning and Boatman (1977) hypothesize that a failure in the mother–daughter relationship leaves the daughter vulnerable to sexual abuse. Therefore, they advocate treatment centering on the mother–daughter dyad. A "humanistic" approach to incest treatment developed by Giarretto (1976) includes multiple treatment modes: individual treatment, mother–daughter therapy, marital therapy, father–daughter treatment, family sessions, group treatment for each family member, and self-help groups. One unifying theme in much of the previous literature is that the occurrence or revelation of sexual abuse presents a family with a crisis that cannot be handled with its usual coping mechanisms. Thus, numerous therapists have advocated an adaptation of classic crisis treatment for handling child sexual abuse (Burgess et al. 1978; Peters 1976; Sgroi 1982; Simrel et al. 1979).

The treatment approach developed by the FCP, drawing on classic crisis theory (Caplan 1964; Lindeman 1944), suggests that crises occur in people's lives when an individual is faced with a major obstacle to achieving important life goals that cannot be surmounted with ordinary coping mechanisms. As the person in crisis struggles ineffectively to apply old problem-solving strategies, she or he experiences increasing discomfort and helplessness, which may reach disorganizing proportions. However, during this period of mounting tension, the individual may be especially accessible to treatment strategies that focus on the quick development of new problem-solving approaches. Thus, crisis intervention not only may relieve the individual's current distress, but may also modify and strengthen his or her capacity to withstand future stresses.

In sexual abuse situations, the assumption is generally made that the occurrence or the revelation of the sexual activity is the precipitant for some type of crisis in the family. The family's usual patterns of coping are disrupted by both the realization that their child has been victimized and the flurry of activity that often ensues as police or protective service workers attempt to investigate the allegations of sexual abuse. The goal of treatment is to restore equilibrium in each of the family members and to help them develop more adaptive coping mechanisms (especially when the sexual abuse has occurred within the family unit).

169

Crisis theory (Caplan 1964) suggests that these goals are best met by intervening as soon as possible after the crisis situation develops. The objective is to engage the patient in the therapeutic work while she or he is most accessible to change. In crisis intervention, no attempt is made to alter basic personality structure. Treatment is brief and focused very specifically on helping to resolve the crisis at hand. Therapists take much more active roles than is customary in psychodynamic therapies. Sessions may be scheduled more often than once a week and may take place in settings other than the therapist's office. The therapist may intercede on the patient's behalf to help him or her resolve a practical problem (for example, obtaining emergency social services or a restraining order against the perpetrator).

Intervention Programs for Victims and Their Families

The FCP treatment model incorporated several of these fundamental tenets of crisis therapy into the crisis intervention aspect of the treatment. As stated above, less than one-quarter of the families seen required only crisis intervention. Most needed more long-term individual or group treatment after the initial crisis intervention.

General Concepts

The FCP has conceptualized the effort needed to help sexually abused children and their families in a model that offers comprehensive clinical intervention and cooperation with all of the other appropriate agencies and systems involved. This model includes a four-pronged approach to the problem.

Investigation

Investigation, substantiation, and case management performed by the state agency responsible for child welfare are the basis for any intervention geared to helping sexually abused children and their families. Most states mandate reporting abuse incidents to that agency.

Clinical services

Clinical services may be necessary at any stage of contact with sexually abused children and their families and are described in greater detail below.

Judicial system involvement

Cooperation between the judicial and mental health systems is becoming increasingly important. Many states are in the process of reassessing their response to child victims from a child welfare as well as from a judicial point of view. In Massachusetts, a 1983 law (General Laws of Massachusetts) mandates reporting incest and serious sexual or physical abuse to the district attorney's office. The decision about whether to prosecute is made at a multidisciplinary conference, which ideally includes the mental health clinicians involved with the child and his or her family. Clinicians are also expected to provide written and verbal testimony in court and to be expert witnesses.

Advocacy

A sexual abuse program has to be involved in a broad range of activities related to the issue. These include 1) consciousness raising with the public, the legislature, and health care and human services providers on the existence and prevalence of the problem of sexual abuse of children; 2) increasing awareness of the problem in the legislature to improve funding for programs and to promote enactment of laws easing the victim's course through the legal system; 3) education regarding prevention, in schools, to groups of health care and human services providers, and through the media; 4) education of the public, especially parents and health care providers, regarding presenting symptoms, elucidation of suspicions, and the most helpful responses to revealed abuse; and 5) coordination of services for the individual families involved with the program, including medical, psychiatric, protective, legal, educational, and foster placement services as well as advocacy on their behalf.

Countertransference Issues

Clinical work with sexually abused children, their families, and offenders can be very stressful; crisis intervention in general requires a high level of activity and involvement; in addition, sexual abuse intervention raises a host of powerful feelings, ranging from disgust and rejection to identification with the victim or the aggressor, and from rage and retaliatory wishes to vicarious and unconscious sexual excitation. Disbelief, minimization, and denial of the occurrence of abuse may represent attempts by the clinician to deal with his or her own feelings, but they have powerful deleterious effects on the presenting victim and family. Countertransference responses tend to become increasingly inappropriate as clinician burnout increases, and lead to ineffective or harmful interventions.

Safeguards against unbearable stress and burnout need to be debated and then incorporated into the concept delineated. Suggestions offered here cannot be exhaustive, as particulars such as case flow, number of staff, levels of expertise, and personal as well as interpersonal dynamics vary.

Teamwork is essential. The seductive power of incestuous family dynamics can easily overcome one clinician's evaluation or treatment of a family system. Team members need to remind each other that mental health professionals are trained to help people acknowledge their feelings, express them, and use them in appropriate ways. Clinicians are not police investigators, child protective workers, prosecuting or defending attorneys, or judges. Interprofessional cooperation and teamwork are crucial, and boundaries are best kept clearly defined.

Clinical Services

The services offered by the FCP include the following:

1. Elucidation of the allegation by clinicians trained to elicit information from children of all ages, developmental stages, and levels of psychological functioning. Staff are experienced in the use of adjuncts such as anatomically correct dolls, doll houses, and drawings.
2. Assessment of the immediate impact of the abuse and its revelation on the child and the family, including the risk for retaliation, further abuse, or psychologic harm as consequences of the revelation. History gathering (prior abuse or neglect in the presenting family or in the background of any family member) is a critical component of the risk assessment.
3. Diagnostic assessment of the child, all family members involved and the offender, leading to *Diagnostic and Statistical Manual of Mental Disorders (Third Edition—Revised)* (American Psychiatric Association 1987) diagnoses, if applicable.
4. Diagnostic assessment of the family dynamics as they pertain to the occurrence of abuse and the risk of reabuse.
5. Medical exam, if indicated, by a pediatrician experienced with sexually abused children.
6. Determination of the kind of intervention or therapy needed based on all the factors listed above. This includes the development of a comprehensive treatment plan for all family members involved, including the offender when applicable.
7. Referral to and consultation with other specialty units for further assessment or treatment.
8. Short- or long-term therapeutic intervention tailored to the needs of each child and family: crisis intervention;

short-term individual, sibling, or couples therapy; group therapy (for latency age and adolescent victims, for mothers of incest victims, and for fathers or grandfathers who committed the incest); and family therapy when appropriate.

9. Periodic reassessment and termination of therapeutic intervention when individual and family goals have been met.

Therapy with an incest or sexual abuse victim and his or her family cannot and does not exist in a vacuum. Cooperation and consultation with other agencies involved are crucial and include the following: working with child protective workers (who in most states have case management responsibilities) investigating the allegation of sexual abuse or offering services after substantiation; working with the judicial system in the form of verbal or written reports and testimony; and providing guidance and support to those victims and families who are testifying.

Conclusion

The model program presented here is but one of several. Others are described in the literature (Burgess et al. 1978; Giarretto 1976; Sgroi 1982). As stated above, follow-up data about various kinds of interventions are not available. All interventions therefore should be regarded as experimental. This implies thoughtful and careful application of various models, permitting the best interests of the child to guide the choice of all procedures. Cooperation with other agencies and professionals is mandated and, increasingly, legislated. Thorough knowledge of the evolving state and federal laws regarding child abuse is required. Advocacy is needed to make interventions more accessible in order to protect the child from revictimization by offenders as well as by the medical, protective, and judicial systems. Public and professional education regarding the revelation or early recognition of ongoing sexual abuse is vital. Prevention of child abuse needs to become a national and local priority.

References

American Psychiatric Association: Diagnostic and Statistical Manual of Mental Disorders (Third Edition—Revised). Washington, DC, American Psychiatric Association, 1987

Ball P, Wyman E: Battered wives and powerlessness: what can counselors do? Victimology: An International Journal 2:454–552, 1977–78

Browning D, Boatman B: Incest: children at risk. Am J Psychiatry 134:1–10, 1977

Burgess A, Holmstrom L: Rape trauma syndrome. Am J Psychiatry 131:981–986, 1974a

Burgess A, Holmstrom L: Rape: Victims of Crisis. Bowie, MD, Robert J. Brady, 1974b

Burgess A, Holmstrom L, Sgroi S: Sexual Assault of Children and Adolescents. Lexington, MA, Lexington Books, 1978

Caplan G: Principles of Preventive Psychiatry. New York, Basic Books, 1964

Chapman J, Gates M (eds): The Victimization of Women. Beverly Hills, CA, Sage, 1978

Department of Social Services: Annual Statistics Reports. Boston, MA, Department of Social Services, 1981–84

Dewsbury A: Family violence seen in general practice. Review of Social Health Journal 95:250–294, 1975

Eisenberg S, Micklow P: The assaulted wife: "Catch 22" revisited. Women's Rights Law Reporter 5:138–147, 1976

Eist H, Mandel A: Family treatment of ongoing incest behavior. Fam Process 7:216–224, 1966

Federal Bureau of Investigation: Uniform Crime Reports. Washington, DC, 1972, 1974, 1982

Field M, Field H: Marital violence and the criminal process: neither justice nor peace. Social Service Review 47:221–240, 1973

Finkelhor D: Sexually Victimized Children. New York, Free Press, 1979

Fonseka S: The study of wife beating in the Camberwell area. Br J Clin Pract 28:400–402, 1974

Gates M: The battered woman: criminal and civil remedies. Paper presented at the 130th Annual Meeting of the American Psychiatric Association, Toronto, Canada, 1977

Gayford J: Battered wives. Med Sci Law 15:237–245, 1975

Gelles R: The Violent Home: A Study of Physical Aggression Between Husbands and Wives. Beverly Hills, CA, Sage, 1974

General Laws of Massachusetts: Amendment of Section 51B of Chapter 119, Chapter 288 of Acts of 1983. Boston, MA, 1983

Giarretto H: The Treatment of Father–Daughter Incest: A Psychosocial Approach (DHEW Publication No. 76–30014). Washington, DC, Department of Health, Education, and Welfare, 1976

Gomes-Schwartz B, Horowitz J, Sauzier M: Sexually Exploited Children: Service and Research Project. Washington, DC, Office of Juvenile Justice and Delinquency Prevention, 1984

Green A: Self-destructive behavior in battered children. Am J Psychiatry 135:579-582, 1978

Gutheil T, Avery N: Multiple overt incest as family defense against loss. Fam Process 16:105–116, 1977

Herman J, Hirschman L: Families at risk for father–daughter incest. Am J Psychiatry 138:7–15, 1981a

Herman J, Hirschman L: Father–Daughter Incest. Cambridge, MA, Harvard University Press, 1981b

Hilberman E, Munson M: Sixty battered women. Victimology: An International Journal 2:460–471, 1977–78

Kansas City Police Department: Conflict Management: Analysis Resolution. Kansas City, MO, 1973

Katan A: Children who were raped. Psychoanalysis of School Children 28:443–449, 1973

Kinsey A: Sexual Behavior in the Human Female. Philadelphia, PA, Saunders, 1953

Levinger G: Sources of marital dissatisfaction among applicants for divorce. Am J Orthopsychiatry 36:803–807, 1966

Lindeman E: Symptomatology and management of acute grief. Am J Psychiatry 101:37–45, 1944

Martin D: Battered Wives. San Francisco, CA, Glide Publications, 1976

Mrazek P, Kempe C (eds): Sexually Abused Children and Their Families. Oxford, England, Pergamon Press, 1981

Ochberg F: Victims of terrorism. J Clin Psychiatry 41:73–74, 1980

Peters J: Children who are victims of sexual assault and the psychology of offenders. Am J Psychother 30:398–421, 1976

Pizzey E: Scream Quietly or the Neighbors Will Hear. Essex, England, Anchorage, 1974

Pizzey E: Chiswick women's aid: a refuge from violence. Review of Social Health Journal 95:297–298, 308, 1975

Ridington J: The transition process: a feminist environment as reconstitutive milieu. Victimology: An International Journal 2:563–575, 1977–78

Rosenfeld A: Incidence of a history of incest among 18 female psychiatric patients. Am J Psychiatry 136:791–795, 1979

Rounsaville B: Theories in marital violence: evidence from a study of battered women. Victimology: An International Journal 3:11–29, 1978

Rounsaville B, Weissman M: Battered women: a medical problem requiring detection. Int J Psychiatry Med 8:191–202, 1977–78

Scott P: Battered wives. Br J Psychiatry 125:433–441, 1974

Seligman M: Helplessness: On Depression, Development and Death. San Francisco, CA, W.H. Freeman, 1975

Sgroi S: Handbook of Clinical Interventions in Child Sexual Abuse. Lexington, MA, Lexington Books, 1982

Simrel K, Berg R, Thomas J: Crisis management of sexually abused children. Pediatr Ann 8:5–11, 1979

Stark E, Flitcraft A, Frazier W: Medicine and patriarchal violence: the social construction of a 'private' event. Int J Health Serv 9:461–493, 1979

Straus M: Leveling, civility and violence in the family. Journal of Marriage and the Family 36:13–29, 1974

Straus M: Wifebeating: how common and why? Victimology: An International Journal 2:443–458, 1977–78

Straus M, Gelles R, Steinmetz S: Behind Closed Doors: Violence in the American Family. New York, Anchor Press/Doubleday, 1981

Symonds M: The psychodynamics of violence-prone marriages. Am J Psychiatry 38:213–222, 1978

Tsai M, Feldman-Summers S, Edgar M: Childhood molestation: variables related to differential impacts on psychosexual functioning in adult women. J Abnorm Psychol 88:407–417, 1979

Waites E: Female masochism and the enforced restriction of choice. Victimology: An International Journal 2:525–534, 1977–78

Walker L: Battered women and learned helplessness. Victimology: An International Journal 2:535–544, 1977–78

Walker L: The Battered Woman. New York, Harper & Row, 1979

Walker L: The Battered Woman Syndrome. New York, Harper & Row, 1984

Washington, D.C., Police Foundation: Police Foundation Report. Washington, DC, Police Foundation, 1983

Chapter 10

Special Intervention Programs for Child Victims of Violence

HOWARD B. LEVY, M.D.
STEPHEN H. SHELDON, D.O.
JOHN R. CONTE, M.D.

Chapter 10

Special Intervention Programs for Child Victims of Violence

It appears that America has been having a love affair with violence. Indeed, concerned professionals and lay public alike have become increasingly frightened and disturbed by the magnitude of reports of violence in this country. Most distressing has been the disproportionate increase in cases of intrafamily violence, especially violence directed at children.

Straus et al. (1980) have reported that Americans are more likely to be murdered in their homes by members of their families than anywhere else or by anyone else. They have also reported that 1.4 to 1.9 million children between 3 and 17 years of age are vulnerable to physical injury by their parents (Gelles 1982; Straus et al. 1980). These numbers are by no means inclusive and reflect only those cases that are identified and enter the "system."

Acts of force against children are not new. They have been recorded throughout history (DeMause 1974). During this past century, organizations dedicated to the prevention of child abuse and neglect, in conjunction with specific government and private agencies, have developed and initiated efforts to provide protection for children. As we enter the mid-1980s, it is important that we recognize that child abuse and other child maltreatment issues have had the benefit of visibility, national recognition, and prototypal legislation. Even so, adequate protection of children from

Reprinted with permission from Brunner/Mazel, 19 Union Square, New York, NY 10003.

acts of violence remains an unfulfilled promise. In spite of increasing involvement on the part of social service agencies, law enforcement and medical communities, and our court systems, charges are frequently made that access to safeguards and services for children and their caretakers remains difficult and discouraging. Service provision often appears fragmented, poorly coordinated, and discontinuous. There remains a sense that individual children and their families become lost within a system that tends to shuffle people among separate service units.

This "system" is a composite of professional groups that include social service, medical, judicial, law enforcement, and mental health disciplines. Each discipline has a specific role in responding to violence and interacting with other members of the community. It is the availability and coordination of these independent systems, as they respond to victims and perpetrators of violence, that define the nature and parameters of a community response to violence.

This chapter first describes the roles, interrelationships, interdependencies, and foibles of various community agencies as they currently exist. A review of the inadequacies in each discipline that result in a potentially less than optimal response also is presented. A theoretical basis for community intervention using known risk factors is suggested, stressing the proactive nonstatic nature of these "vulnerability" factors. Following this theoretical matrix, a coordinated community response is delineated. Last and most important in terms of long-range strategies for the future is a discussion of further policy development and research.

The Systems Approach to Intervention

Identification and Reporting

Entry into the system of potential responses to family violence is dependent on the identification of the child abuse victim and the subsequent report of that episode to the mandated state protection agency. The report is the trigger for the subsequent cascade of responses.

Each state has a child abuse reporting law that stipulates that certain professionals *must* report all cases of suspected child abuse and neglect to that state's child protection agency. Failure to report places the mandated professional at potential risk for civil liability. Those professionals designated as mandated reporters vary in each state but usually include physicians, teachers, social workers, and police officers. Child abuse reports are not limited to mandated reporters, however, and may be initiated by anyone who suspects that a child has been or is being abused. Once a report of abuse has been generated, an investigation is begun to determine whether the allegation of abuse is valid. Evidence is gathered from interviews with the child's caretakers, other family members, neighbors, and involved professionals. An appraisal of the child's home environment is also undertaken and assessed in terms of safety and adequate resources.

The report and subsequent investigation process are complex, and their outcome can be affected by variations in the levels of knowledge, skill, and commitment of mandated reporters, nonmandated reporters, and Child Protection Service (CPS) investigators. The child victim must therefore rely on the competence of the reporter and investigators. Adding to this potential confusion are the vastly different manifestations of child abuse and neglect. Signs and symptoms of abuse may relate to the specific area of the child's body that has been traumatized or may be symbolic. An example of the latter is the acute onset of bed-wetting in a previously toilet-trained child who has sustained multiple inflicted bruises. Because children have a limited ability to defend or protect themselves against injuries, they may exhibit subtle personality or behavioral changes as sequelae to the violence they have sustained. A not infrequent example in this area is the deterioration in school performance of a child who has been sexually abused.

The investigation of a report of suspected child abuse usually involves interviews with the alleged victim and her or his family as well as the presumed abuser. Collateral interviews with neighbors or other professionals frequently occur simultaneously. As part of this information-gathering process, children are often interviewed and examined by physicians, although in many states this unfortunately is not a routine aspect of all child abuse investigations. Interviews typically occur in the child's and the family's environment (for example, home, school, or neighborhood).

Training of investigators varies greatly between and even within states. Most states have deprofessionalized the CPS job classification so that prior social service or mental health education is not a requirement for job eligibility. Few states have developed detailed investigative guidelines or protocols, and policies vary greatly across states. This lack of standardized procedure appears to have resulted in a situation in which there is considerable individual CPS worker discretion in the handling of cases. More important, the accuracy of CPS decisions is an issue of considerable debate among professionals and one that suffers from a lack of empirical investigation.

Once a case of suspected abuse is founded or determined as having some validity by the investigation, a number of other systems are activated.

Law Enforcement

The primary function of law enforcement is to investigate allegations of violations of the law and to gather evidence that may be used to prosecute those who break the law. This function is designed to protect society and the victim from additional illegal acts. The function of the police in gathering evidence includes interviewing crime victims and witnesses and collecting physical evidence. The different types of intrafamily violence result in significant variations in the extent to which victims are capable of providing a statement about their victimization, whether or not there are available witnesses who can corroborate what the victim has said, and/or the presence of physical evidence. An example of the variation in victim capability is illustrated by the sexually abused two-year-old child who may not have the language skills to describe his or her abuse. In spite of these difficulties, increasing experience suggests that in the majority of reports of intrafamily violence police are able to obtain the information required to take further action.

Once a report is made to the police they initiate an investigation to determine whether there is credible evidence that a crime has been committed. This determination involves assessing victim and witness statements, collecting physical evidence, and assuring that the chain of evidence remains intact. In cases of intrafamily violence police are allowed broad discretion about which steps to take immediately. Depending on the circumstances, they may arrest the offender, take temporary custody of child victims, or refer adult victims to temporary shelters. In some jurisdictions, perpetrators of intrafamily violence may be contacted by telephone and asked to come to the police station for booking. If victim advocates are available the police may be able to call upon them to help shepherd victims through the intervention process. These and other services help the police carry out their primary function of investigating crime while minimizing additional trauma to victims.

Justice System

The justice system consists of the law enforcement and court subsystems (civil and criminal courts). Generally, each of the justice subsystems is charged with the broad mandate of protecting society from illegal acts. However, without an actual violation of the law, the justice system is prohibited from entering into the private lives of citizens. Interpersonal violence between strangers is almost universally regarded as an appropriate focus of justice system concern, but there is no such agreement about the role of the justice system in responding to the violent home. Interpersonal violence between members of the same family is often regarded as a "family matter" in which the state should not intervene. The arguments for and against justice system involvement are often emotional and pragmatic (Conte 1984).

Our assumption is that acts of interpersonal violence within a family must be responded to by all of the systems charged to deal with interpersonal violence. Failure to respond in a coordinated fashion places victims of intrafamily violence at a disadvantage relative to victims of extrafamily violence. Moreover, in dealing with violence committed within the family the justice system may respond, but in a different manner than it does in cases involving extrafamily violence. The manner and sensitivity with which the justice system responds to intrafamilial violence will determine the appropriateness of intervention by this discipline.

After a police report has been made and an investigation has begun, two separate aspects of the justice system are often engaged.

Criminal justice system

The criminal justice system, which is responsible for *protecting society* through the prosecution and punishment of those who break the law, may be involved depending on the type of crime and identity of the perpetrator. Criminal law stipulates that acts of sexual assault, battery, and physical assault are against the law, but the specifics of what constitutes criminal (in the family setting) rather than civil law violations vary across jurisdictions.

In criminal law proceedings, although the victim is an interested party, his or her role is primarily that of a witness. Criminal justice proceedings are often criticized because of their apparent insensitivity to and lack of concern for the needs and rights of victims. Even though the primary function of the criminal justice system is the prosecution and punishment of offenders, there is an increasing awareness that the criminal justice system may also be used to encourage offenders to enter treatment.

The use of the criminal justice system as a means to encourage offenders to accept responsibility for their actions and to receive treatment that is aimed at reducing their potential for continued criminal behavior is hotly debated. Those who oppose the use of the justice system to force offenders into treatment argue that one cannot "treat a crime," that it is impossible to coerce behavioral changes, and that forcing perpetrators into treatment denies them their rights to due process. Those who favor the use of the justice system to force offenders into treatment stress that many offenders have no insight into their behaviors and rationalize their acts of violence. For example, the sexual abuse of a child is explained as a means of teaching that child about sexuality. The psychologic distortions associated with most acts of intrafamily violence require some mechanisms to help the offender understand the illegal and harmful nature of his or her behavior. In many cases no alternative is available to replace the justice system as a mechanism for helping offenders accept responsibility for their. behavior and enter treatment.

Civil justice system

Civil justice involvement in cases of intrafamily violence has the primary function of *protecting the victim*. Child protection investigations of reports of child abuse or neglect are mandated in every state. Although in some jurisdictions the police may be mandated to investigate reports, each state also has a child protection agency that must investigate all reports and take steps to protect the child. The mandated agency must also provide services to attenuate the conditions that were responsible for the child's injury. In many states a case of reported child abuse or neglect must be validated before any social service may be provided to the child or family. When a child is judged to be at serious risk, CPS may take temporary custody of the child and place him or her in a safe environment. This may involve placing the child with other relatives or in a foster home.

The civil justice system also includes the juvenile court, which has the long-term responsibility of protecting the child and must often approve the plans formulated by the state social services department. Occasionally the juvenile court may also stipulate services designed to alter the conditions that required removal of the child from his or her home. This branch of the civil justice system is responsible for the legal termination of parental rights in those cases where it is determined that this action will be in the child's best interest. Civil justice action also may be helpful through the use of *no-contact* orders, by which perpetrators of violence are ordered out of the home and are not to have contact with other family members. Usually these orders stipulate a specific period of time.

Regardless of which aspect of the justice system is involved in intrafamily violence, there is increasing agreement that such involvement should be as sensitive and atraumatic as possible. Numerous innovations have been implemented to reduce the likelihood that this intervention will be a significant source of trauma in the lives of victims of intrafamily violence (Conte and Berliner 1981). These diverse innovations include teaching justice system personnel about the dynamics of interpersonal violence in order to lessen their misconceptions about family violence; training police and attorneys to be sensitive interviewers of victims of violence; reducing the number of times victims are required to repeat the story of their victimization; vertical prosecution, which allows the same prosecuting attorney to handle a case throughout its legal proceedings; whenever possible, removal of the offender rather than the victim(s) from the home; and pretrial or postconviction diversion programs that offer treatment as an alternative to incarceration.

Social Services

The social services comprise a wide range of specific interventions that are designed to prevent or alleviate social problems or contribute to their solution. These services also are intended to improve the well-being of individuals, groups, and communities. They may be provided by both private (voluntary) and government agencies. Although the scope of services varies in each community, they usually include financial supports such as food stamps and Aid to Families with Dependent Children, subsidized housing, homemaker and visiting nurse services, emergency food and clothing, temporary shelters, and job training.

These supports can provide essential ingredients in professional efforts to prevent and ameliorate the impact of intrafamily violence. An example of this is the use of homemakers as a means of keeping children safe and at the same time avoiding the costs of out-of-home care in neglect cases. Income, housing, and food supports can significantly reduce the stress that parents may be experiencing and that also appears related to many acts of physical child abuse. The availability of temporary shelters supplemented by emergency food and other supports makes it possible for women to protect themselves and their children from violence. These services offer women an option other than remaining in an abusive environment simply because they have no other means of financial survival. Job training and income supplements make it possible for mothers to support their families and improve their living conditions. These supplements may be pivotal factors in a process that reduces parent vulnerabilities associated with family violence. Although the availability of these services should reflect the measurement of user need, they are often available only to those cases identified as being at the most serious risk. Furthermore, various legislative changes have resulted in an absolute decrease in the availability of these services (L. Brown, personal communication, 1984).

Mental Health

Mental health services encompass a continuum of specific interventions and also are designed to remediate specific behavioral aspects of individuals, families, or small groups that may be associated with intrafamily violence. Until recently there has been some distrust of mental health approaches since many mental health practitioners have tended to treat all intrafamily violence as an intrapsychic problem and the product of intra- or interpersonal variables. This view might dictate that the stress resulting from inadequate housing, food, or other basic life-sustaining resources be treated with counseling rather than by helping the client obtain adequate support. The theoretical framework outlined later in this chapter suggests that violence may be the result of a number of vulnerabilities. Some of these vulnerabilities reside within individuals or families, while others reside in communities or are the result of state and federal policy decisions.

Recognition that intrafamily violence is the result of a number of interactive variables suggests that mental health services can be useful in many cases of interpersonal violence. These services often include skill training such as parent training that teaches parents nonaversive child management techniques; parent education to increase parent knowledge of child development and nutrition; stress management classes; advocacy training/availability, in which therapists either advocate or teach clients those advocacy skills necessary to obtain their own goods and services; or individual, small group, or family therapy.

Medicine

It was not until the 1940s that physicians noted the specific association of healed fractures and chronic subdural hematomas in young children (Caffey 1946). Less than a decade later, Silverman published an article recognizing that these injuries appeared to be the result of repeated nonaccidental traumas (Silverman 1953). Although radiologists were at the forefront of medicine's involvement in the diagnosis of child abuse, it was not until Dr. C. Henry Kempe and his associates coined the term "battered child syndrome" that the medical profession became active in the area of child abuse and neglect intervention (Kempe et al. 1962). In spite of the medical community's late entry into the system of community response, it is often in a unique position to protect the child and maintain a therapeutic liaison with the family or caretakers. The physician reporter is unusual in the community system of interventions in that there is no burden placed upon him or her to validate a report or to win a case, to gain a conviction, or to obtain adequate information needed to incarcerate a perpetrator. The physician, by nature of his or her training, seeks only to be an advocate for the child and family. The doctor may therefore be able to avoid the pitfalls and handicaps of many of the other community intervention services.

The physician not only functions as a mandated reporter using his or her diagnostic intervention skills, but also can provide acute treatment for any existing injuries. In addition, he or she may also be able to lay the foundation for any future rehabilitation of the child and his or her caretakers.

Unfortunately, in spite of their potential role as gatekeepers to the system, physicians are at times hesitant to report their suspicions of child maltreatment. They often lack adequate information related to child abuse and are inexperienced in handling these emotionally charged situations. These difficulties are frequently related to the inadequacy of preparatory curricula relating to family violence in medical schools.

Inexperience and limited medical school coursework, however, are only two of the factors contributing to physicians' reluctance to report. Other issues that affect physician involvement are hesitancy to believe that violent acts against children can possibly be perpetrated by family

191

members whom the physician has known over a period of years; hesitancy to become involved in judicial proceedings; disinclination to take time from a busy practice to provide court testimony; and fear of confronting the perpetrator (Helfer 1975). Recent information suggests a continued belief of physicians that the "system" may be more disruptive than helpful, and emphasizes a perception by physicians that after they initiate a report they will be unable to obtain any follow-up.

Nonetheless, the physician is often pivotal in gaining valuable information through the medical interview of the child and/or the caretaker, as well as from the subsequent examination and laboratory tests. The physician must ultimately be able to translate his or her knowledge of child development and the family as a unit with the physical examination and laboratory tests into a community treatment plan. The thoroughness and completeness of the interview, the examination, and the ability to collate this information may be exceedingly important to the outcome of the case. Unfortunately, the information needed to assess cases of intrafamily violence may be unfamiliar to the physician. This is especially true for those physicians involved in very technical or specialized areas of medicine. Lack of experience with the results of child abuse, other than those directly related to the injury, may result in the physician's acting in a very pragmatic manner. Under such circumstances he or she may provide only acute treatment for the specific injury brought to his or her attention. In addition, confusion over certain aspects of reporting laws, exemplified by the word "suspicion" as it is used in child abuse reporting, may result in physician underreporting. These issues are exacerbated by the array of community services and networks that often confuse the physician. Many physicians are left with a sense of lack of accomplishment and are frustrated in attempts to shepherd their patients and their families through these systems.

Gaps in Knowledge

In spite of the vast number of research projects studying violence and its sequelae, several areas have not been adequately addressed. These gaps in our knowledge preclude any truly efficient or viable response to the problem of handling cases of violence and child abuse.

Although the more holistic interest in violence within the home is relatively new, there is an expanding research effort. This effort is likely to alter how professionals view the origins, effects, and ideal treatments of all types of family violence. Unfortunately, much of this research takes place within disciplines, and there is little cross-fertilization between professional disciplines. Overall, research and other activities focusing on any one type of violence have had little influence on other types of violence. Consequently, professionals concerned with physical child abuse are often not aware of developments in child sexual abuse. Neither group tends to be aware of the development with children touched by domestic violence.

Several major gaps in current knowledge strike us as the most pressing in terms of community responses to the violent home.

What Is the Etiology of Violence?

Most experts concur that exposure to discord, violence, and lack of resources are common elements in the background of individuals who become perpetrators of abuse and/or neglect. The exact etiology or imprinting pattern has remained elusive. It remains unclear if these factors must occur at a finite point in time, in a specific sequence, or over a predetermined duration. Adding to this confusion is the question of why an individual perpetrates neglect (as opposed to sexual abuse or physical abuse) and not necessarily the same type of violence to which he or she had been exposed.

193

Much of the research on the origins of violence has tended to focus on a single type of violence (for example, child abuse or sexual violence) and on a limited number of variables. We suggest that a multivariable approach may more profitably identify the set of variables associated with the various types of interpersonal violence. While it is likely to be some time before a single model of the genesis of violence is developed and validated, research that quantifies the variables will significantly contribute to understanding the occurrence of violence. Research directed at the correlations between various risk factors is likely to be of immediate utility in planning organized responses to violence.

What Is the Prevalence of Child Abuse and Neglect?

There is still an uncertainty as to the actual incidence of violence directed at children, and this reflects a lack of definition as well as the varying sensitivities and knowledge of reporters. Research thus far has led most investigators to believe that the abuse and neglect of children are underreported, but the magnitude of underreporting is still unknown. As alluded to earlier in this chapter, one of the major factors in underreporting rests with the lack of education and comprehension of abuse and neglect by both mandated and nonmandated reporters. A prime example is the lack of understanding by some physicians that failing to recognize and report abuse may lead to more serious harm of a child. A second example is the damage that comes from a CPS worker unfounding a case because it lacks sufficient evidence for legal action, when the "lack of evidence" is actually due to the worker's failing to understand another discipline's role or jargon. These disparities emphasize the need for a systems approach to child abuse and neglect reporting.

What Are the Physical Findings in Child Sexual Abuse?

A previously underemphasized area has been the incidence

of physical abnormalities present in victims of intrafamilial sexual abuse. Several investigators have found a moderate degree of crossover abnormalities—physical injuries present in victims of sexual abuse that are distinctly different from the known sequelae of the sexual molestation. For example, it remains unclear as to the actual incidence of concomitant physical abnormalities occurring in cases of incest. The significance of sexually transmitted diseases in young children is only now becoming appreciated as they relate to the pervasiveness and varieties of transmittable illnesses. Only recently has *Chlamydia trachomatis* been recognized as an important disease of sexual origin in young children. The extent of this entity's potential role in the subsequent infertility of infected children is unknown, as is the question of whether it is transmitted with any frequency by a nonsexual route in children beyond infancy. Furthermore, the potential ability of laboratories to provide information about *Chlamydia*, subtyped in a strain-specific fashion and cultured from the victim and the perpetrator, poses stimulating legal and medical issues. In addition, methods are now available to detect evidence of prior *Chlamydia* infection even after the host has been adequately treated.

In part, problems with sexually transmitted diseases in children are confusing and underrepresented because of state confidentiality laws. A requirement that these laws be qualified for young children is now more appreciated than previously.

How Best to Treat Violence?

Currently, there are few data that describe the effects of various services to either the victims of violence or the perpetrators. Decisions about which clients are best served and with which services are currently based on clinical experience or occasionally are based on the biases of individual social service workers. Perhaps more important, it is not clear that violent individuals who receive a package of services will benefit as measured by a reduction or elimination of their potential to commit further acts of violence. Concomitantly, while we know that physical wounds of violence do heal, it is not clear that the psychologic consequences of interpersonal violence can be healed by any intervention without substantial scarring.

In an age of declining service dollars, knowledge about what types of services, for what types of clients, producing what kinds of effects, and how long these effects last strike us as fundamentally important. Society is no longer willing to "throw money" at problems. Therefore, any argument for spending money to reduce the problem of violence would be significantly strengthened if proponents were able to provide data supporting the assumption that intervention does produce a positive outcome.

How Does a Community's Response to Violence Actually Operate?

One of the most interesting issues surrounding a community's response to the violent home is the extent to which the response conforms to the ideal model that the community describes. We are unaware of any data describing how a community actually handles violence. Although community response involves interagency agreements designed to ensure coordination and integration across agencies, there is no evidence that these systems actually provide such responses. Similarly, we know of no data that describe a client's movement through the various systems or the consequences of the various systems' decisions about the client.

The latter is typified by our paucity of understanding as to what happens to abused children when police or CPS workers fail to take protective custody. How many of these children are ultimately reabused? How many are reabused in the time period shortly after the failure to take custody? Limited data, generated mainly by the medical community, are available, but they show only that nonreporting statistically places these children at significant risk for further and more serious injury (Fontana and Besharov 1979).

There are specific questions regarding how various subsystems operate and how the entire community response system actually functions. Although poorly handled cases are occasionally identified by one or another system in a community, it is not clear whether mishandling is an exception or a rule in most communities. Nor is it clear what happens to most cases of abused children who are identified. For example, in Cook County, Illinois, where a special sexual abuse unit has been formed to investigate cases of sexual abuse, there has been an increase in the percentage of "founded" cases to over 70 percent of the more than 1,365 cases reported in 1983. However, the state of Illinois is able to provide financial support for the treatment of only a fraction of these cases. What happens to the remaining cases of sexually abused children identified by CPS is unknown at this time. Our knowledge base is in danger of remaining incomplete until some mechanism is developed to share information and improve communication among professionals.

Theoretical Basis for Community Intervention

The literature is replete with descriptions of risk factors for family violence and child abuse. Many cite the interplay between various factors including cyclical violence (that is, children who grew up in a violent environment and experienced child abuse are more likely to grow up to be child or wife abusers), socioeconomic status, social stress within families, and social isolation (Gelles 1982). Others have cited factors intrinsic to the child that are instrumental in child abuse, including prematurity (Maden and Wrench 1977), low birth weight (Park and Collmer 1975), handicaps, retarded or delayed development (Steinmetz 1978), congenital defects, psychomotor retardation, hyperactivity, chronic illness (Thompson 1983), and children whose parents perceive them as different from other children (Steinmetz 1978). Lastly, certain environmental factors are considered instrumental in the development of violence toward children, such as large family size (Straus et al. 1980), lack of parental attachment to child, low job satisfaction, alcohol abuse, and economic stresses (Gelles 1982; Levy and Sheldon 1984).

It must be noted, however, that none of the factors cited have been proven to be absolute predictors of child abuse or neglect. Child abuse is an interactional event (Kadushin and Martin 1981) combining risks and vulnerabilities of the host, agent, and environment. Garbarino (1982) discusses the concept of vulnerabilities rather than risk as being an earlier determinant in child maltreatment. He states, "The vulnerable parent is one who need not become high risk unless conditions conspire to exploit or attack the parent. It is on the foundation of vulnerability that risk is built by environmental circumstances" (p. 45).

Upon the foundation of vulnerabilities Garbarino describes, we have developed a theoretical matrix to assess the likelihood of abuse in a given family over time. If proven functional, it will provide a practical basis for community intervention in the violent home.

Child abuse events do not appear to be isolated phenomena (Kadushin and Martin 1981). They are stimulated by events that cascade into violent interactions. Most experts agree that there is a constant and varying interaction among the child, parents, and environment that may lead to abuse or neglect. Most descriptions of this dynamic milieu include only one or two dimensions. An ecologic paradigm, however, requires a four-dimensional analysis. The role of the child in the genesis of abuse is well supported in the literature. From the earliest parent–child interaction, the child is responsible for shaping and modifying parental behavior according to the child's behavioral, genetic, and emotional makeup. Children (even the youngest infant) exhibit characteristics that are additive to the vulnerability of the situation. Some of these vulnerabilities include prematurity, behavior disorders, sleep disturbances, and congenital defects (see Table 1). Parental vulnerabilities might include a recent separation or divorce, economic hardship, aggressive personality, low self-esteem, and dependency (see Table 2). The child's vulnerabilities can exacerbate a parental vulnerability, increasing tension and interpersonal stress. Conversely, a lack of vulnerabilities may defuse a potentially violent interchange. The environment, composed of the people, services, mores, values, and beliefs within the family's neighborhood, town or city, society, and culture, also has its vulnerabilities, which exist concomitantly with the parent's and the child's vulnerabilities. These include sanctioned corporal punishment, poverty, unemployment,

TABLE 1. Child's Vulnerability Factors

1. Hyperactivity
2. Prematurity
3. Low birth weight
4. Low IQ
5. Colic
6. Demanding
7. Withdrawn
8. Acquired defect
9. Congenital defect
10. Genetic abnormality
11. Chronic illness
12. Low satisfaction with family life
13. Difficult, irritating behavior
14. Tense, high strung
15. Increased intensity of reactions
16. Irregularity of reactions and behavior
17. Indifferent
18. Adopted
19. Dependent
20. Emotional unresponsiveness
21. Habits which get on parent's nerves
22. Separation
23. Tantrums
24. Nightmares
25. Sleep disturbances
26. Child seen as worse than others

TABLE 2. Parental Vulnerability Factors

 1. Anxiousness
 2. Aggressiveness
 3. Suspicious of others
 4. Dependent
 5. Less able to seek support from others
 6. Less nurtured as child
 7. Poor understanding of parenting
 8. Does not encourage reciprocity with child
 9. Frustration of dependency needs
10. Psychopathology
11. Low self-esteem
12. Low satisfaction with family life
13. Depression
14. Impulsiveness
15. Identity problems
16. Low intelligence
17. Self-centered
18. Marital strife
19. Frequent job changes
20. Alcoholism
21. Abused or neglected as child
22. Looks to children to satisfy own needs
23. Jealousy
24. Inability to deal with child's needs
25. Inappropriate demands on child
26. Lack of knowledge of child development
27. Expectations too high for developmental level of child
28. Lack of consistent positive reinforcement
29. Use of extremes of physical punishment
30. Easily upset or angry
31. Use of threats and complaints
32. Use of broad range of discipline techniques
33. Single parent
34. Young parent
35. Less frequent interactions with child
36. More negative interactions with child
37. Separation of parent and child
38. Poor health
39. Recent separation or divorce
40. Economic hardship

lack of assistant housekeeping services, and lack of agency supports (see Table 3). In addition to the child's vulnerabilities, the concreteness of the parental strength, the presence or absence of a vulnerable environmental milieu, and time determine the degree of modification of the parent.

Our framework depicts the three interacting and overlapping spheres of parents, child, and environment existing within and being affected by a neighborhood, town, society, and culture—the ecological unit (see Figure 1). The spheres are constantly changing their characteristics and degree of influence, resulting in a dynamic interaction of variables. The smaller spheres revolve within two larger ones: the society and the culture in which the family exists.

Characteristics of the child, the parents, and the environment may be placed on separate axes of a three dimensional model (see Figure 2). A matrix may then be established containing eight separate cells in three dimensions. The spheres of family, individuals within the family, environment, culture, and society reside within the matrix.

Environmental vulnerability factors are placed on the x axis, child vulnerabilities on the y axis, and parental

TABLE 3. Environmental Vulnerability Factors

---

 1. Sanctioned use of force in society
 2. Separation
 3. Unstable marriage
 4. Divorce
 5. Unemployment
 6. Poverty
 7. Lack of agency supports
 8. Inability to seek supports
 9. Child labor
10. Young marriage
11. Children thought of as property
12. Sanctioned corporal punishment
13. Social isolation
14. Absent extended family
15. Cultural practices of brutality as initiation rites
16. Lack of assistant housekeeping services

---

vulnerabilities on the z axis. Therefore, environmental factors move the ecologic unit from right to left within the matrix, child factors move the unit from top to bottom, and parental factors move the unit from front to back. The construct assumes a dynamic nature of interrelationships. Constantly the ecologic unit is changing and segments are influencing each other. These interactions vary from time to time,

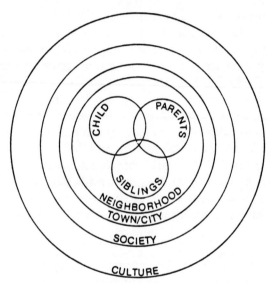

FIGURE 1. The family as an ecological unit.

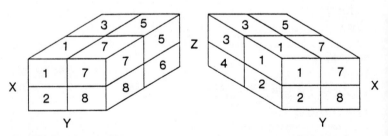

FIGURE 2. Environmental (x), child (y), and parent (z) vulnerabilities to child abuse.

202

resulting in fluid movement between cells. At an isolated point in time, the position within the cells might be identified. With the addition of the variable of time, the direction of movement might be approximated. When vulnerability factors are qualitatively added to the construct (+ meaning the presence of vulnerability factors and − meaning the absence of vulnerability factors), the cells may be defined as in Table 4.

Situational analysis may then predict that a violent act against the child would most likely occur when the ecologic unit approaches or lies within cell 6 in which all vulnerability factors are present. The risk would be high when the unit lies within cells 4, 5, or 8, and the direction of movement is toward cell 6. Cells 2, 3, and 7 represent lower risk while the lowest risk for a violent event would occur in cell number one. If quantification of vulnerability factors could be established, the mathematical location of the ecologic unit could be determined. When time is added to the construct, the direction of movement might also be elucidated. If velocity and acceleration could be approximated, a mechanism for quantitative analysis of a family unit and their vulnerability could be designed. This would provide a reproducible mechanism for accurate diagnosis.

The community provides the cultural and social spheres within which the ecologic unit revolves. If accurate diagnosis can be made, community resources must be available to impact on the vulnerabilities. Intervention must come from within the defined spheres; external interventions, that is, those outside of the spheres requiring modification, are generally ineffective in dealing with those variables within the spheres.

Implications for Research, Service, and Social Policy

This chapter has suggested a number of points relative to how communities do and should respond to violence against children. Some of these points have their origins in empirical work; others are an outgrowth of direct practice in community settings, responding to the victims and the perpetrators of violence. As we review this chapter several major areas stand out as the most important in thinking how things might be different for children.

TABLE 4. Analysis of Environmental Vulnerability Factors

Cell	Definition	Analysis
1	c− p− e−	*Lowest risk cell:* Absence of all vulnerabilities.
2	c+ p− e−	*Low-risk cell:* The vulnerable child is in a nurturant, low-risk environment with strong parents exhibiting minimal vulnerabilities.
3	c− p+ e−	*Low-risk cell:* The vulnerable parent is in a supportive environment and the child manifests minimal vulnerabilities.
4	c+ p+ e−	*High-risk cell:* The vulnerable parent is faced with a difficult child who manifests his or her own significant vulnerabilities. However, the environment is supportive. With minimal change in environmental factors, an abusive or neglectful event may occur.
5	c− p+ e+	*High-risk cell:* Parental vulnerabilities are high and the environment is not supportive. However, the child is *not* manifesting behavior or characteristics that might precipitate an abusive event.
6	c+ p+ e+	*Highest risk cell:* Parental vulnerabilities are high, as are the child's. The environment is not supportive and the risk of a violent act occurring is great.
7	c− p− e+	*Low-risk cell:* Parent's and child's vulnerabilities are minimal. Though the environment is not supportive, parent's and child's strengths reduce the risk of a violent event.
8	c+ p− e+	*High-risk cell:* The child manifests significant vulnerabilities, and the environment is not supportive. The absence of violent acts relate to the concreteness of parental strengths. Minimal changes in the vulnerability of the parents might precipitate a violent act.

Note. c = child; p = parent; e = environment

Multivariable Matrix

Considerable empirical work to date suggests that there are a number of factors associated with violence within the home. These variables have been identified in a host of research studies addressing the specific aspects of violence in individual family members and communities. Much additional empirical work is still needed to understand the specific combination of intraindividual, interpersonal, and community variables associated with the various types of violence. Current knowledge supports the matrix suggested previously in this chapter as an organizing framework.

Service Implications

Preliminary as it may be, the matrix suggests a number of specific service interventions that can potentially reduce the vulnerabilities associated with violence within the home. While many of these interventions are of unproven significance, there is sufficient reason to assume that some are in fact change-producing enough to warrant further investigation.

Violence Is the Problem of the 1980s

Every statistic supports the belief that interpersonal violence is the problem of the 1980s. The direct cost of violence in terms of individual and social responses to injury and the disruption of individual and family life, combined with the costs of intervention by various professionals, has not been calculated. It is likely that it may be beyond meaningful comprehension. The indirect costs in terms of suffering, lost potential, decrease in productivity, and allocation of some of the assumed costs of violence (for example, juvenile delinquency) is likely to be incalculable.

Implications for Research, Service, and Social Policy

Our focus in this discussion of the implications of the issues we have raised is on those issues that can be responded to in the immediate future. Our intent is to discuss those issues that can potentially result in practical actions to reduce violence against children.

Research

The call for more research is almost obligatory in a chapter such as this. As pressure for available funds has significantly increased in the last five years, federal and state funding for research has dramatically decreased. This has resulted in a situation in which the very real needs of abused children and their families must be weighed against the need to understand more about the causative factors. The battle this creates between service providers and researchers is unfortunate. It strikes us as an indication that the survival of individual groups and the preservation of turf may be more important than the desire to reduce violence. Although we are mindful of competition for funding those activities that impact on the suffering of children and their families versus the longer range research activities useful in preventing future suffering, we believe there are a number of research activities of immediate concern.

Cost of violence. Calculating the cost of violence in terms of the direct and indirect consequences is likely to require considerable creativity. Nevertheless, if reasonable cost-estimating procedures can be developed, the forthcoming information will be extremely helpful in making future social policy decisions concerning the reduction of family violence.

Empirical description of the community's response. As described previously in this chapter, there are clear ideas about how community systems should respond to the violent home. What remains unclear is whether present community responses conform to the existing models for coordinated interagency actions. It is also unclear whether the systems actually perform their roles as described in these models. Practical research is needed that describes the manner and consequences of the way communities actually handle cases of violence against children. This research should identify those factors that support and those that impede the operation of a coordinated, victim-sensitive community.

Outcome studies. Few data are available concerning the power of individual or aggregate interventions to actually reduce the incidence of violence against children. Although there are a number of potentially effective intervention strategies, few available data support the actual effectiveness of these interventions. As the pressure for existing funds increases, it is likely that available research monies will be diverted to interventions that have demonstrated effectiveness.

Etiological research. In terms of developing long-range strategies directed at decreasing violence against children, additional research on the causes and factors associated with the development and maintenance of violence is essential. Much of the research to date has focused on a limited set of variables, which often reflect only individual or intrafamily variables. The matrix outlined earlier in this chapter suggests that etiological research addressing a wider range of individual, familial, and community variables may be more successful in identifying factors associated with the development of violence.

Services

A need for more services to violent homes is apparent, but such services may remain unavailable for the foreseeable future, in light of the present budgetary constraints and priorities. Decisions about which services should be offered to violent homes are hampered by the lack of data describing the effects of those various services. Equally problematic is the general lack of understanding about how the current social service and mental health service delivery systems actually operate. It is imperative that as we are faced with fewer available services, we develop an efficient and compassionate method of selecting clients and assuring access. Presently, access to services appears to be based more on the individual discretion of social service workers than on any organized plan within the social service departments of most states. This state of affairs suggests a number of implications:

Investigative protocols. Most state social service departments limit their policies and procedures to investigative formats (for example, how soon after a report is filed an investigation must be concluded or what specific forms must be completed by what date). A more productive approach might be to determine which factors should be considered in investigating a report of violence against a child. Most notably missing in many CPS investigations is a systematic assessment of psychosocial variables (for example, vulnerabilities thought to be associated with the risk for violence). The development of assessment strategies that incorporate these risk factors and the subsequent training of CPS workers to conduct such assessments are likely to be quite helpful in the early identification of cases at risk for more serious violence.

Decision-making criteria. Although there are few data describing the operation of the multidisciplinary community response system, experience suggests that this system often operates in a capricious manner. Variations in individual case decisions are determined more by which worker has the case than by any internal aspects of the case itself. It appears that cases are often handled in a manner that violates good case management principles and community-developed models. This state of affairs suggests that detailed decision-making criteria should be developed and employed by each system. These criteria should assist each system in making appropriate decisions and ensure that cooperation and coordination across systems actually occur.

Many communities have also found that the establishment of multidisciplinary review teams to periodically review case decisions can be helpful in improving the operation and efficiency of the community's response to these cases. This concept should be expanded to allow individual workers to request consultation from these review teams and external experts, as well as to periodically identify difficult cases for review.

Policy

The implementation of any policy intended to reduce the incidence of violence against children will require substantial efforts to alter the present trends of our federal and state policymakers. It is mandatory that our legislators understand that further reductions in social and economic supports for children and their families are counterproductive and possibly catastrophic. The recognition that violence against children is the result of a number of factors is implicit in developing a compassionate and practical solution. The vulnerabilities that appear to be related to violence against children cannot be resolved by establishing computerized central registries. These registries identify cases of abuse but are unable to provide the necessary services needed to reduce or eliminate the risk to children and their families.

Perhaps more fundamentally, society must make essential decisions about whether it is willing to carry out those activities that are likely to reduce the vulnerabilities associated with abuse. Recent history suggests that society may not be willing to make that commitment.

References

Caffey J: Multiple fractures in the long bones of infants suffering from chronic subdural hematomas. American Journal of Roentgenology 56:163–173, 1946

Conte JR: The justice system and sexual abuse of children. Social Service Review 58:556–568, 1984

Conte JR, Berliner L: Prosecution of the offender in cases of sexual assault against children. Victimology 6:102–109, 1981

DeMause L: The History of Childhood. New York, Harper & Row, 1974

Fontana, VJ, Besharov DJ: The Maltreated Child. Springfield, IL, Charles C. Thomas, 1979

Garbarino J: Healing the social wounds of isolation, in Child Abuse. Edited by Newberger EH. Boston, Little, Brown, 1982

Gelles RJ: Child abuse and family violence: implications for medical professionals, in Child Abuse. Edited by Newberger EH. Boston, Little, Brown, 1982

Helfer RE: Why most physicians don't get involved in child abuse cases and what to do about it. Children Today 4:28–32, 1975

Kadushin A, Martin J: Child abuse as an interactional event, in Child Abuse: An Interactional Event. Edited by Kadushin A, Martin J. New York, Columbia University Press, 1981

Kempe CH, Silverman FN, Steele BF, et al: The battered child syndrome. JAMA 181:17–24, 1962

Levy HB, Sheldon SH: A hospital's response to the increasing incidence of child abuse and neglect in an inner-city population. The Mount Sinai Journal of Medicine 51:161–165, 1984

Maden MF, Wrench DF: Significant findings in child abuse research. Victimology 2:196–224, 1977

Park RD, Collmer CW: Child abuse: an interdisciplinary analysis, in Review of Child Development Research (Volume 5). Edited by Heatherington M. Chicago, University of Chicago Press, 1975

Silverman FN: The roentgen manifestations of unrecognized skeletal trauma in infants. American Journal of Roentgenology 69:413–427, 1953

Steinmetz SK: Violence between family members. Marriage and Family Review 1:1–16, 1978

Straus MA, Gelles RJ, Steinmetz SK: Behind Closed Doors: Violence in the American Family. New York, Anchor Press, 1980

Thompson M: Organizing a human service network for primary and secondary prevention of the emotional and physical neglect and abuse of children, in Child Abuse and Neglect: Research and Innovation. Edited by Leavitt JE. The Hague, the Netherlands, Martinus Nijhoff Publishers, 1983

Chapter 11

Community Prevention Programs in Family Violence

MARY LYSTAD, Ph.D.

Chapter 11

Community Prevention Programs in Family Violence

Mental health research in the last 20 years has focused on a number of aspects of family violence. Early studies concentrated on problems of child physical abuse; more recent studies have included a focus on wife battering and on sexual abuse of children and of wives as well. Findings of these research studies show that family violence is more likely to occur when the individual is unable to fulfill his or her emotional needs in the family or in other support groups, when the social group situation makes it easy to commit violence, and when the culture itself condones the act (Finkelhor 1979; Lystad 1975, 1983; Straus et al. 1980).

This chapter describes the theoretical concepts and empirical research on the causes of family violence. It then focuses on community prevention measures as they relate to known causes of the problem. Community prevention programs in family violence are for the most part new and untested; it is important to share knowledge now about those that seem to work and to carefully evaluate what they are accomplishing.

Causes of Family Violence

If the function of the family is to love, to nurture, and to support its members, then violence in the family is incompatible with its function. Why does it occur? Theories of the causes of family violence have changed considerably over time. In some of the early clinical discussions of the problem, the female victim and her psychologic makeup were blamed. She was purported to fantasize the attack, wish for the attack, enjoy the attack, and/or was too weak to protect herself from attack. Only recently has the offender been looked at carefully as an individual person and also as a collective of persons who aggress against those in less powerful positions, viewing this behavior as their right. The social–structural and cultural factors in justifying large-scale victimization of women and children are just beginning to be studied in depth.

Three behavioral causes of family violence are examined in detail below. The first cause involves psychologic needs and development as they relate to interpersonal violence between individuals. The second cause involves those social statuses and structures that encourage family violence. The third cause involves cultural attitudes and values that legitimize violence in the family and in societal institutions.

Psychologic Causes

Psychologic studies of violence in the family have been looked at in terms of individual competency and coping skills and in terms of demands and pressures on the individual. In the first instance, some studies indicate the aggressor more often suffers from psychologic disorders: personality disorders, maladaptive behaviors, and psychoses, including manic depressive and schizophrenic behavior (Bennie and Sclare 1969; Elmer 1971; Grumet 1970).

Zalba (1966), in analyzing child battering by schizophrenic parents, states that parents act out or displace their anger over marital conflicts onto their children. Children become convenient targets of abuse and injury in the process of displacement, with the adult denying intrapsychic stress and other hostility and aggression.

Alcoholism and drug abuse frequently accompany male aggressive behavior. Spouses, in particular, tend to reject the offender because of their disgust at the alcoholism and its

216

consequences. Alcohol also lessens the offender's inhibitions against committing violence (Awad 1976; Fontana 1971; McCord 1979).

In terms of demands and pressures on the individual, some researchers have found that child abuse is related to the stress of mothering. Elmer (1971) and others point out that child abuse is usually the result of accumulated stresses within the family and that these stresses occur most frequently in the lower socioeconomic classes. Among the stress-producing factors are the birth of several children close together, premature birth, and special physical or emotional problems incurred by children. With the increasing isolation of the nuclear family from relatives, and with the increasing number of one-parent families, parents, most often mothers, are on call 24 hours a day, seven days a week, 52 weeks of the year. When there is no relief from the pressures of this job, stresses can result in aggression of one sort or another.

Walker (1979) writes that social learning theories yield considerable information consistent with available empirical and clinical findings. In these theories violence is seen as learned aggressive behavior that is continually reinforced as the individual grows up. Novaco (1977) reports on successful training programs that deal with anger and conflict management.

Further study of psychologic causes of family violence should focus on the basic emotional needs of family members. What are such needs? What is the role of the family in responding to such needs? What is the interplay (or lack of interplay) of the family with other social institutions in responding to such needs? From such a perspective one may ask further questions on how the frustrations and stresses on the individual of economic insecurity, community isolation, illness, and overwork contribute to child abuse and to violence between husband and wife, and why there is violence rather than passive withdrawal or some other mode of displacement.

Social Causes

Explanatory models that rely solely on the factors of psychopathology and intrapersonal stress are not sufficient to a full understanding of the problem; certain social values are also significantly correlated with the occurrence of violence. Among the significant social characteristics of the offender are his childhood socialization, his position in the family, and his position in the society.

A number of studies of physical assaults in the family identify a generational pattern of abuse: The battered child tends to become a battering adult. Social scientists have long recognized that patterns of child rearing, both good and bad, are passed on relatively unchanged from one generation to the next. This phenomenon can be described as an identification with the aggressive parent, an identification that occurs even though the offspring may strongly wish to be different (Jenkins et al. 1970; Lascari 1983; Oliver et al. 1971). The social experience of being a victim of sexual abuse as a child appears to be a factor in whether or not one becomes a sexual abuser (Groth and Hobson 1983; Swift 1977).

The power structure within the family is also a factor in offender behavior. Gelles and Straus (1979) and Steinmetz (1980) relate violence of husbands to wives to the traditionally superordinate–subordinate relationships of men and women and of adults and children found both in the family and in other societal groups as well. Children are even less able than adults to avoid abuse. Finkelhor (1979) argues that children do not know enough about psychosexual development or needs to define the situation as abusive. Because of their low-power status, they are helpless to ward off the abuse. Finally, the social position of the offender in the larger society appears to relate to violent behavior. Lower socioeconomic status (using educational, income, and occupational indices) has been shown to be significantly correlated with family violence (Julian and Mohr 1979; Straus et al. 1980;

Zuckerman et al. 1972). Straus found further that the most intense violence occurs in households in which the husband is unemployed or employed part-time. In his national sample, unemployed men were twice as likely as fully employed men to use severe violence on their wives. Men employed part-time had a rate of wife beating three times the rate for men employed full-time. Further, unemployed men and men employed part-time were three times more likely to be beaten by their wives. Children whose fathers were employed part-time were nearly twice as likely to be victims of severe violence as were children whose fathers held full-time jobs.

McCall and Shields (1986) point out American social systems' uneasiness in their approach to revising norms regulating use of force, that is, their grave ambivalence regarding capital punishment, police brutality, and corporal punishment in schools, prisons, and the military. Revising norms limiting the use of force within the almost sacred institution of the family seems particularly troubling to the American public. Yet, as Lerman (1986) points out, recent demonstration projects have increased the use of formal criminal charges in domestic assault cases. Through close coordination with mental health agencies, and through the development of extensive victim services, prosecution has become an appropriate and a desirable legal remedy for many domestic assault cases. Lerman also views diversion or deferred prosecution as a viable alternative to traditional criminal case processing. In such instances prosecution is suspended while a defendant completes a counseling program; successful completion of the program results in a dismissal of charges.

There is a need for study of the changes in relationships between individuals in the family and changing relationships of the family with support institutions such as the church, school, and work. Not only new family forms, but the restructuring of old forms should receive attention. Of particular importance is the study of the child-rearing function in our society. Who is to care for the child, attend to his or her physical needs, socialize him or her, teach him or her? Who is to love the child?

Cultural Causes

A number of researchers have looked at the society itself and the values it holds that condone violent behaviors. Two values are singled out in the literature: the value of male superiority and the value of physical force as a problem-solving device. Mokran and Kramer (1976) and Steinmetz (1977) relate the historical roots of male dominance to violence against women in American and other cultures. Perpetrators of violent acts are described as having personality traits of dominance and aggression; they feel it is acceptable to abuse physically and sexually, since they are males and leaders in society. Further, young boys in general have been socialized to such roles, and young girls have been socialized to be passive and to accept such male behavior.

Because of male dominance in society, some women acquiesce to the notion that wife battering of a sexual or other nature is all right because the wife belongs to the husband. According to Walker (1979), such women feel powerless to make their wishes and needs known, and they accept male violence. They may stay in the home because of economic, legal, and social dependence, and may feel that alternative living arrangements are unacceptable. Many daughters similarly accept sexual abuse because they do not feel they have any other rights or choices.

Abrahamsen (1970) and Gil (1970) discuss the attitudes and values of cultures that sanction violence as a way of life. Gil writes that the reason for considerable child abuse in American society is that the cultural norms of child rearing allow the use of a certain amount of physical force toward children by the adults caring for them. Use of force is encouraged by the mass media and particularly by television, which, in both adult- and child-centered shows, frequently and provocatively project violent behavior (National Institute of Mental Health 1982).

There is also a need to know more about ascribed roles for male and female children at home, in school, and on the playground, which encourage competence and self-esteem. There is a need to know more about the effects of mass-media images of male and female roles, as well as its images of violence as acceptable means to ends.

Community Intervention/Prevention Programs

The community intervention/prevention programs outlined below derive from what is known about the nature of family violence. Their goal is to assist the family and other social institutions (education, legal, and medical) that support the family. These programs include public education efforts directed to parents and teachers, innovative changes in legal and medical procedures for assisting the family in need, and efforts to change opportunities, values, and expectations for all members of the society.

Programs Focused on the Individual

1. Educational programs for teenagers and young adults, dealing with family functioning and child care: In addition to learning algebra and geometry, young persons need to be informed about the needs of the family, about the problems that may arise in meeting these needs, and about age-appropriate behaviors of children. Classes currently offered in community mental health centers, YMCAs/ YWCAs, and church groups often address these needs.
2. Skill building for teenagers and young adults in anger and conflict management: In the first phase of this mental health approach, participants begin to learn to identify the situational cues that arouse their anger, including perceptions of others' intentions, imminent pain, or personal injury or loss. The second phase involves skill acquisition,

221

teaching the ability to reinterpret the anger-arousing situation in ways that reduce or eliminate the angry response. The third phase is application and practice; the procedures used are essentially those of desensitization.

3. Special help to families with mentally ill and substance abusing members: Since these families are more vulnerable to family violence, especially to child abuse, it is crucial that the members be made aware, by social service agencies serving them, of alternative ways of working out frustrations and anxieties.

4. Interpersonal networks for nuclear families: Without the traditional supports of the extended family, small families, especially if they are one-parent families, need outreach— in the apartment building, on the block, or in the church. Support networks allow a spouse or parent time to get away from the family as well as time to talk to someone about common family problems.

Programs Focused on the Social System

1. Education of educators in the rights and responsibilities of children in social and physical interactions in the classroom and on the playground: Children are socialized in the school as well as in the home. Teachers need expertise in providing role models of nonviolence and in explaining clearly what is acceptable behavior and what is not acceptable behavior toward peers.

2. Increased opportunities for men and for women who want to work outside the home: American society places high value on the salaried work ethic. A person's dignity and self-esteem are often related to his or her position in the workplace. All persons need to have available work training and work opportunities commensurate with their abilities and goals in life.

3. Increased use of formal criminal charges in domestic assault cases: Prosecution of offenders is a just and desirable legal resource for many victims of violence. It

should be used along with mental health services for victims. Innovative programs emphasize the importance of enforcement of court orders, penalties, and rehabilitative measures.

4. Increased use of diversion or deferred prosecution as an alternative to traditional criminal case processing. Diversion of domestic violence cases provides a means of obtaining control over a group of defendants who have largely eluded criminal justice intervention. The leverage obtained over batterers admitted to a diversion program may be used to require participation in a mental health counseling program focused on stopping violence and/or substance abuse.

Programs Focused on Cultural Values

1. Strong public advocacy for nonsexist roles and responsibility in the family: Women with children should not be expected to stay at home all the time and be denied stimulating activities outside of the home. Nor should the fathers of children be deprived of pleasures and rewarding responsibilities of child care. The women's movement, with help from concerned men, has had considerable impact nationally in changing sex role images, but more must be done.

2. Sensitization of parents (mothers, fathers, stepparents, and grandparents) to the need of female as well as male children for positive self-images of themselves, including respect for one's personal space as well as the personal space of others and the ability to say no to intrusions: As long as girls and boys are treated differently from the time of birth, in terms of the cultural artifacts given to stimulate them (guns for boys, dolls for girls) and in terms of the demands made on them (heavy competition in sports for boys, politeness for girls) there will be male offenders and female victims in and out of the home. Parent discussion groups, with help from women's groups, are very useful.

3. Reduction in the frequency and intensity of violence displayed in the mass media: The American culture of violence—from television war stories and crime shows for adults (which children watch) to cartoon violence for children—has been discussed repeatedly, but little has changed. Crimes of violence are presented on television, in popular magazines and comic books, and elsewhere as legitimate and exciting ways of controlling people. Retribution through violence is also extolled. Public demand for a change is essential.

4. Establishment of national victims rights groups: Women's advocacy groups in the area of child abuse, sexual abuse, and battered women can be looked to as models for the development of a victim's rights movement in this country. The President's Task Force on Victims of Crime (1982) and the Attorney General's Task Force on Family Violence (1984) are recent, important examples of federal and local ventures into defining the problems and identifying effective ways in which family violence can and should be addressed. There is a need for more groups to provide public education that speaks not only to the negative outcomes of family violence but to the positive effects of proper family interactions and conflict resolution.

Obviously, conceptually sound and well-meaning prevention programs need evaluation. What is helpful for what populations? How do you reach the groups more vulnerable to violence? How do you integrate family and school supports with overall mass-media advocacy for prosocial behaviors? Prevention studies are expensive and answers do not come easily. But with available knowledge about the dynamics of family violence it is important to encourage and evaluate prevention programs now.

The prevention measures mentioned here are not all inclusive. Some are further reaching than others. Could they be accomplished in this decade? Certainly not by a single federal program, nor even by the cooperative efforts of mental health professionals who have a crucial educational role as well. They can only be accomplished by an American public sufficiently incensed by the problems of family violence to act upon heightened feelings of outrage. Many Americans esteem "the family" as a sacred and cherished institution. It is this value and this sense of caring that provide hope for the future.

References

Abrahamsen D: Our Violent Society. New York, Funk and Wagnalls, 1970

Attorney General's Task Force on Family Violence: Final Report. Washington, DC, Department of Justice, 1984

Awad G: Father–son incest: a case report. J Nerv Ment Dis 162:135–139, 1976

Bennie E, Sclare A: The battered child syndrome. Am J Psychiatry 125:975–979, 1969

Elmer E: Child abuse: a symptom of family crisis, in Crisis of Family Disorganization. Edited by Pavenstedt E. New York, Behavioral Publications, 1971

Finkelhor D: Sexually Victimized Children. New York, Free Press, 1979

Fontana V: Which parents abuse children? Medical Insight 3:16–21, 1971

Gelles R, Straus M: Determinants of violence in the family: toward a theoretical integration, in Contemporary Theories About the Family. Edited by Burr W. New York, Free Press, 1979

Gil D: Violence Against Children: Physical Child Abuse in the United States. Cambridge, MA, Harvard University Press, 1970

Groth N, Hobson WF: The dynamics of sexual assault, in Sexual Dynamics of Anti-Social Behavior. Edited by Revitch E. Springfield, IL, Charles C. Thomas, 1983

225

Grumet B: The plaintive plaintiffs: victims of the battered child syndrome. Family Law Quarterly 4:296–317, 1970

Jenkins R, et al: Interrupting the family cycle of violence. Journal of the Iowa Medical Society 60:85–99, 1970

Julian V, Mohr C: Father–daughter incest: profile of the offender. Victimology: An International Journal, 4:348–360, 1979

Lascari A: The abused child. Journal of the Iowa Medical Society 62:229–232, 1972

Lerman L: Prosecution of wife beaters: institutional obstacles and innovations, in Violence in the Home: Interdisciplinary Perspectives. Edited by Lystad M. New York, Brunner/Mazel, 1986

Lystad M: Violence at home: a review of the literature. Am J Orthopsychiatry 45:328–345, 1975

Lystad M: Sexual abuse in the home: a review of the literature. International Journal of Family Psychiatry 3:3–31, 1983

McCall G, Shields N: Social and structural factors in family violence, in Violence in the Home: Interdisciplinary Perspectives. Edited by Lystad M. New York, Brunner/Mazel, 1986

McCord J: Etiological factors in alcoholism: family and personal characteristics. Quarterly Journal of Studies on Alcohol 33:1020–1027, 1972

Mokran A, Kramer R: Incest and incestuous behavior in forensic practice. Cesk Psychiatr 72:320–323, 1976

National Institute of Mental Health: Television and Behavior: Ten Years of Scientific Progress and Implications for the Eighties (DHHS Publication No. (ADM) 82-1195). Washington, DC, 1982

Novaco R: A stress innoculation approach to anger management in the training of law enforcement officers. Am J Community Psychol 5:327–346, 1977

Oliver J, Taylor A, et al.: Five generations of ill-treated children in one family pedigree. Br J Psychiatry 119:473–480, 1971

President's Task Force on Victims of Crime: Final Report. Washington, DC, 1982

Steinmetz S: The Cycle of Violence: Assertive, Aggressive, and Abusive Family Interaction. New York, Praeger, 1977

Steinmetz S: Women and violence: victims and perpetrators. Am J Psychother 34:334–350, 1980

Straus M, et al: Behind Closed Doors: Violence in the American Family. New York, Doubleday, 1980

Swift C: Sexual victimization of children: an urban mental health center survey. Victimology: An International Journal 2:322–327, 1977

Walker LE: The Battered Woman. New York, Harper and Row, 1979

Zalba S: The abused child: I. A survey of the problem. Social Work 11:3–16, 1966

Zuckerman K, Ambuel J, Bandman R: Child neglect and abuse: a study of cases evaluated at Columbus Children's Hospital in 1968–69. Ohio State Medical Journal 68:629–632, 1972

Conclusion

LEAH J. DICKSTEIN, M.D.
CAROL C. NADELSON, M.D.

Conclusion

Citing the "overwhelming evidence that violence in television programming can have a negative and severe behavioral impact on young people and adults," Dr. Melvin Sabshin, Medical Director of the American Psychiatric Association, has written to U.S. Senator Paul Simon (D-Ill.) supporting the Senator's draft legislation to address the problem of televised violence through the cooperative efforts of television networks and their affiliates (Sabshin 1987).

In 1985 the Family and Children's Agency of Metropolitan Louisville experienced a 10 percent increase in requests for assistance. Family violence headed the list of major presenting problems (Family and Children's Agency of Metropolitan Louisville 1985).

A bulletin-board poster at the University of Louisville Counseling Center reads

> "Domestic Violence Is a Deadly Cycle"
> Women and men are needed to volunteer through the Local YWCA Spouse Abuse Center to help those caught in this repetitive cycle of stress, violence and making up that can grow deadlier with each episode. You can:
> —Be a hospital advocate
> —Be a court advocate
> —Answer the 24-hour crisis hotline
> —Be a public speaker
> —Work with children at the Center

On "60 Minutes" (March 20, 1988) a special report concerned some Brazilian men's supposed defense of their honor, termed *machismo*, by abuse of "their" women, even to the point of murder. In the November 15, 1985, issue of *Psychiatric News*, an article entitled "Women Kill Their Spouses to Stop Abuse" included data from a study by Drs.

231

Drs. Corbin Johnson and Bun Tee Co that suggested that women kill their husbands for different reasons from why husbands kill their wives, that is, to stop chronic abuse rather than because of perceived rejection (Johnson and Co 1986).

Under a law that took effect January 1, 1986 in California, physicians, podiatrists, and most other health practitioners are required to report actual or suspected abuse of dependent adults including elderly dependent adults. Reports must be made whenever there is reasonable cause to suspect abuse is present, including physical or mental abuse, sexual abuse, neglect, intimidation, deprivation of nutrition or medical care, financial abuse, or other forms of mistreatment. Reports must be made to an adult protective service agency or a law enforcement agency and are confidential (Action Report 1986, p. 1, 4).

Each year over one million children feel the pain of child abuse and over 2,000 children each year die from child abuse. The December 28, 1986, *New York Times* quoted from the *Journal of Pediatrics*, which described a new test to uncover hidden cases of child sexual abuse. Drs. Jeanne McCauly and Richard L. Gorman, at the University of Maryland, applied a dye to the outside of the vaginal tissue of children and adolescents within 48 hours of an abuse incident. They reported that as many as 80 percent of victims who showed no signs of physical trauma on examination revealed detectable skin breaks with the applied dye (McCauley and Gorman 1986).

Health professionals who are employed by a public or private agency, health facility, clinic, or other facility must read and sign a statement acknowledging awareness of this requirement as a condition of continued employment. The statement reads:

> Section 15630 of the Welfare and Institutions Code requires that any care custodian, health practitioner, or employee of an adult protective services agency or a local law enforcement agency who has knowledge of or observes a dependent adult

in his or her professional capacity or within the scope of his or her employment who he or she knows has been the victim of physical abuse, or who has injuries under circumstances which are consistent with abuse where the dependent adult's statement indicates, or in the case of a person with developmental disabilities, where his or her statements or other corroborating evidence indicates that abuse has occurred, report the known or suspected instance of physical abuse to an adult protective services or a local enforcement agency immediately or as soon as practically possible by telephone and to prepare and send a written report thereof within 36 hours of receiving the information concerning the incident.

To gain insight into the size of this problem of elder abuse, we need only look at New Jersey statistics of an estimated 53,000 victims reported by the New Jersey Advisory Council on Elderly Abuse (New Jersey Advisory Council on Elderly Abuse 1986).

In June 1986, Connecticut Governor William A. O'Neill signed into law a family violence bill that ranks among the strongest in the nation. Under the law, Connecticut becomes the seventh state to require an arrest in cases of probable domestic assault, whether or not the victim is willing to sign a complaint. This new law is linked to Tracey Thurman of Torrington, Connecticut, a 21-year-old estranged wife who was shot and left permanently partially paralyzed as a result of spouse abuse. While increased awareness and protection are available to family violence victims, continued prevention programs and treatment options are needed because the National Institute of Justice Study released in July 1986 cited these grim statistics:

1. More than 1.7 million people each year face a spouse with a gun or a knife.
2. About 2 million annually are beaten by their spouses.
3. Over eight percent of the 18,692 homicides in the United

States in 1984—1,570 victims—involved one spouse killing another (Meddis 1986).

October 1, 1987 marked the beginning of National Domestic Violence Awareness Month in the United States. At the same time the fact may not be well known that battering is the number one cause of injury to women (Burkett and McNamara 1987).

These examples of current attention to the problems of family violence probably represent thousands of others across the nation. From a historic perspective paleopathologists at the Virginia Commonwealth University's Medical College of Virginia have detected what appears to be evidence of spouse abuse among 2,000- to 3,000-year-old mummies of pre-Columbian men and women in Chile and Peru. The incidence of skull fractures was much higher among females, 60 percent in one group, and 45 percent of these cases were labeled fractures secondary to lethal blows from personal violence since there was no known war in progress at that time (Medical News 1986, p. 11).

Theodora, famed Byzantine empress (A.D. 508-548), ruled equally with Justinian. She initiated many reforms on behalf of women, never forgetting the suffering and humiliation she saw women endure during her youth when she was an actress. Among her most important accomplishments was ensuring the prevention of physical abuse of women by their husbands (Chicago 1980).

The authors in this volume are nationally recognized experts in the field of family violence and represent the majority of professions currently involved in this devastating social problem of the 1980s. These fields are medicine, including psychiatry and pediatrics; psychology; social work; education; law; and the police system. From the theories, policies, clinical material, and research data, it is evident that current and future work in this field must be based on a multidisciplinary approach if family victims and victimizers are to be helped in a crisis and in avoiding future repetitious events.

An increasingly accepted dictum is the need to view one current incident of family violence as a possible correlate to other current or remote actions and reactions of abuse or victimization in other possibly multigenerational family members (Hawton 1985). For example, Dr. Jean Goodwin writes,

> As we understand more about the interconnected cycles of violence in families, it becomes apparent that each intervention is preventive at multiple levels. Thus the helpful intervention in the family of the abused elder may not only prevent further elder abuse, but also spouse abuse or child abuse by other family members. (Goodwin 1985)

The point can be extended to identify other less frequently mentioned, though very helpless, victims of family violence, namely, the physically and emotionally handicapped, whose care may often increase family stress and, in fragile situations, precipitate violence. For instance, more professionals are aware of the incidence of multiple personality disorder among children, adolescents, and adults. This disorder, primarily the result of family violence, whether incest, physical or psychologic abuse, occurs most commonly among women. If questioned, patients will readily divulge their hidden and denied histories of family violence.

A sociologist at Northwestern University, Netta Gilboa, uses slides of the media portrayal of violence against women in pornography and advertising to raise consciousness about this form of subtle as well as explicit but often unrecognized violence against women. Her examples range from record album covers of half-naked women to shoe advertisements as well as graphic scenes of bondage, rape, and the worst of the hard-core magazines reserved for adult bookshops (Abraham 1985).

The data from prevention programs begun in the past two decades make it clear that the destructive effects of stereotypic sex-role socialization for women and men play major roles in the etiology of family violence. Although there have been many changes, there continue to be major differences in the sex-role socialization of men and women that may contribute to the violence we have discussed. Women continue to be encouraged to be more dependent, men are discouraged from developing nurturing skills, and there continues to be a use and abuse of direct and indirect power by both sexes.

If they have not done so before, it is incumbent upon health professionals to assume primary responsibility to inquire about possible instances of family violence from every patient/client with whom they interact, regardless of age, gender, marital status, socioeconomic, racial, religious, ethnic, geographic, and educational group. In addition, information concerning access to and possession of handguns and other lethal weapons must be sought. As with incest, rape, alcohol abuse, sexual, and other personal problems, unless we professionals ask specific questions, our patients will continue to feel too guilty or unaware of their importance to divulge this history. Requesting this information in a supportive manner to decrease fear, shame, and guilt, as well as to identify these experiences as important, will enable referrals and treatment to become active and common options.

In addition to the superb work of programs at spouse abuse shelters like My Sister's Place in Washington, D.C., and at centers for abusers like Emerge in Boston, support and educational networks for prevention must be organized at places of employment and in all schools, from nursery to graduate levels, along with general health services.

Recognition of family violence plus the establishment of primary, secondary, and tertiary prevention and treatment programs are our responsibility. The authors in this monograph reiterate this fact. Many people, victims, victimizers, other family members, and professionals alike, do not always recognize or even choose to recognize the violence and the existence of this definable and overwhelming problem.

Among many potential and currently unanswered research questions implicated in interpersonal violence are

1. To what extent is violence portrayed in the media incorporated into real lifestyles of the vulnerable?
2. What effect does the modeling of family violence through the use of spanking and other forms of corporal punishment have upon the psyche of children and adults?
3. How effectively are the spouse and child abuse reporting laws complied with?
4. How comprehensive are the state child and spouse abuse reporting laws for physicians, nurses, other allied health workers, teachers, social workers, police officers, and others?
5. How well coordinated and publicized to the victims and helping professionals are the elder, spouse, and child protective systems?
6. Is there a correlation between battering behavior by men and their real or imagined sexual dysfunction? In one study of 34 men who were batterers, 31 admitted that their wives complained about their husbands' sexual inadequacies (Harris 1986).

Research is expensive. However, not doing research, and therefore not having useful and insightful data available for program planning and treatment intervention, is more expensive in terms of money *lost* and lives *maimed*.

If, as Dr. Benedek stated, "Violence is a *last* cry for help," then this sign must be recognized and responded to. Finally, as part of a society that has begun to understand family violence, the helping professions must join with self-help groups, governmental agencies, and educational institutions to assume responsibility for helping to change social institutions and child-rearing practices implicated in predisposing people of all ages to family violence.

References

Abraham M: Slide show graphically illustrates violence against women. Louisville Courier Journal, April 7, 1985, pp. 1–2

Abused women get leverage in Connecticut. New York Times, July 15, 1986

Burkett K, McNamara M: The highs, the lows: lasting memories of 1986. MS Magazine 15:19–26, 1987, p. 19

California Board of Medical Quality Assurance Action Report: Adult Abuse Reporting Requirement. 30, 1986, p. 1, 4

Chicago J: The Dinner Party: Needlework, Embroidery, Our Heritage. Garden City, NY, Anchor Books/Anchor Press, Doubleday, 1980

Family and Children's Agency of Metropolitan Louisville: Annual Report 1985 6(2), 1986

Goodwin J: Family violence: principles of intervention and prevention. Hosp Community Psychiatry 36:1074–1079, 1985

Harris RN: Questions and answers. Medical Aspects of Sexuality 20:75, 1986

Hawton K: The risk of child abuse among mothers who attempt suicide. Br J Psychiatry 146:486–489, 1985

Johnson C, Co BT: Women kill their spouses to stop abuse, study presented at AAPL meeting shows. Psychiatric News, November 15, 1986

McCauley J, Gorman RL: Test to uncover hidden cases of child sex abuse described. New York Times, December 28, 1986

Meddis S: Study attacks family violence. USA Today, July 7, 1986

New Jersey Advisory Council on Elderly Abuse. American Medical News, July 11, 1986, p. 27

Sabshin M: Television violence. Legislative Newsletter (American Psychiatric Association Division of Government Relations), July 15, 1987, p. 3

Violence among the ancients. Medical News, December 9, 1986, p. 11

Appendix 1

Bibliography

LEAH J. DICKSTEIN, M.D.

Appendix 1

Bibliography

This is a *topical* bibliography. It includes references which may already be listed in a chapter.

Incest

Cleveland D: Incest: The Story of Three Women. Lexington, MA, Lexington Books, 1986

Fox R: The Red Lamp of Incest. New York, E.P. Dutton, 1980

Goodwin J: Sexual Abuse: Incest Victims and Their Families. Littleton, MA, PSG Publishing, 1982

Herman JL, Hirschman L: Father–Daughter Incest: Understanding Treatment. Boston, Little, Brown, 1982

Renshaw DC: Incest: Understanding and Treatment. Boston, Little, Brown, 1982

Battered Women/Spouse Abuse

Bard M, Sangrey D: The Crime Victim's Book. New York, Brunner/Mazel, 1985

Barnes K: Breaking the Silence. New York, RF Illustrated, An Occasional Report on the Work of and published by the Rockefeller Foundation, September 1986

Beauchamp W (ed): A Private War. Letters and Diaries of Madge Preston, 1862–1867. New Jersey, Rutgers University Press, 1987

Benedek EP: Spouse Abuse: Who Is the Victim? Videotape produced by the Forensic Center, Michigan Department of Mental Health. Directed by Dr. Benedek. New York, Brunner/Mazel, 1985

Bowker LH: Beating Wife-Beating. Lexington, MA, Lexington Books, 1983

Browne A: When Battered Women Kill. New York, Free Press, 1987

Carlin K: Why women first. Aegis: Magazine on Ending Violence Against Women 35:68–74, 1982

Chapman JR, Gates M: The victimization of women. Sage Yearbooks in Women's Policy Studies 3, 1978

Costa JJ: Abuse of Women: Legislation, Reporting, and Prevention. Lexington, MA, Lexington Books, 1983

Ewing CP: Battered Women Who Kill: Psychological Self-Defense as Legal Justification. Lexington, MA, Lexington Books, 1987

Giles-Sims J: Wife-Battering: A Systems Theory Approach. New York, Guilford Press, 1983

Hilberman E: Overview: the "Wife-Beater's Wife" reconsidered. Am J Psychiatry 137:1336–1347, 1980

Michael RP, Zumpe D: An Annual Rhythm in the Battering of Women. Am J Psychiatry 143:637–640, 1986

Okun L: Woman Abuse. Facts Replacing Myths. Albany, NY, SUNY Press, 1987

Pagelow MD: Woman-Battering (Volume 129). Beverly Hills, CA, Sage Library of Social Research, 1981

Reponse to the Victimization of Women and Children. Edited by Chapman JR. Interdisciplinary Journal of the Center for Women Policy Studies, New York, Guilford Press, 1987

Schechter S: In Honor of the Battered Women's Movement: An Appraisal of Our Work. Keynote Address, Second National Conference of the National Coalition Against Domestic Violence, Milwaukee, WI, August 1982

Schechter S: Women and Male Violence: The Visions and Struggles of the Battered Women's Movement. Boston, South End Press, 1986

Shimoff MB: Battered Women: A Problem for the Jewish Community. Women's American ORT Reporter, March/April 1981, pp. 10–12

Legal Issues

Bannon J: Law enforcement problems with intra-family violence. Paper presented at the American Bar Association Convention, 1975

Bolton FG, Bolton SR: Working With Violent Families, a Guide for Clinical and Legal Practitioners. Newbury Park, CA, Sage Publications, 1987

Curran WJ: Forensic Psychiatry and Psychology. Philadelphia, F.A. Davis, 1986

Lerman L: Criminal prosecution of wife beaters. Response to Violence in the Family 4(3):1–19, 1981

Lerman L: A feminist critique of mediation in wife abuse cases. Response to Violence in the Family and Sexual Assault 7(1):5–13, 1984

Maidment S: Domestic violence and the law: the 1976 Act and its aftermath. Sociology Review 31:4–25, 1985

Rosenbaum A: Family violence, in Forensic Psychiatry and Psychology: Perspective and Standards for Interdisciplinary Practice. Edited by Curren WJ. Philadelphia, F.A. Davis, 1986

Schetky DH, Benedek EP: Emerging Issues in Child Psychiatry and the Law. New York, Brunner/Mazel, 1985

Sherman LW, Berk RA: The Minneapolis domestic violence experiment. Police Foundation Report 1, April 1984, pp. 1–20

Tanay E: Family violence. Journal of Forensic Sciences FFSCA 29(3):820–824, 1984

Male Batterers

Adams D: Continuum of Male Controls over Women. Boston, MA, Emerge, 1984

Adams D: Stages of anti-sexist attitude and behavior change for abusive men. Paper presented at the 92nd Annual

Convention of the American Psychological Association, Toronto, August 1984

Adams D, McCormick AJ: Men unlearning violence: a group approach based on the collective model, in The Abusive Partner: An Analysis of Domestic Battering. Edited by Roy M. New York, Van Nostrand Reinhold, 1982

Dobash RE, Dobash RP: Unmasking the provocation excuse. Aegis: Magazine on Ending Violence Against Women 37:57–68, 1983

Newsletter. Emerge, A Men's Counseling Service on Domestic Violence. Available from Emerge, 25 Huntington Avenue, Room 323, Boston, MA 02116

Pleck JH: Men's power with women, other men and society: a men's movement analysis, in The Women Say, The Men Say. Edited by Shapiro E, Shapiro B. New York, Dell Publishing, 1979

Ptacek J: The clinical literature on men who batter: a review and critique. Paper presented at the Second National Conference for Family Violence Researchers, Durham, NH, August 1984

Sonkin D, Martin D, Walker LE: The Male Batterer: A Treatment Approach. New York, Brunner/Mazel, 1986

Child Abuse

Biller HB, Solomon R: Child Maltreatment and Paternal Deprivation. Lexington, MA, Lexington Books, 1986

Braun BG (ed): The Treatment of Multiple Personality Disorders. Washington, DC, American Psychiatric Press, 1986

Brown J, Melinkovich P: Schonlein-Henoch purpura misdiagnosed as suspected child abuse. JAMA 256:617–618, 1986

Burgess AW, Hartman CR: Child abuse aspects of child pornography. Psychiatr Ann 17:248–253, 1987

The child beating years. The Valley Advocate. April 21, 1986, p. 10

Ciba Foundation: Child Sexual Abuse within the Family. Summit, NJ, Ciba Foundation, 1985

Dayee FS: Private Zone: A Book Teaching Children Sexual Assault Prevention Skills. Edmonds, WA, Charles Franklin Press, 1982

DeJong AR: The medical evaluation of sexual abuse in children. Hosp Community Psychiatry 36:509–512, 1985

Epstein N: Top-shelf MD witness wages war on child abuse. American Medical News, March 6, 1987, p. 3

Finkelhor D, Associates: A Sourcebook on Child Sexual Abuse. Beverly Hills, CA, Sage Publications, 1986

Finkelhor D: Child Sexual Abuse, New Theory and Research. New York, Free Press, 1987

Finkelhor D: The sexual abuse of children: current research reviewed. Psychiatr Ann 17:233–241, 1987

Finkelhor D: Sexually Victimized Children. New York, Free Press, 1987

Freeman L: It's My Body and Mi Cuerpa Es Mio. Seattle, WA, Parenting Press, 1983

Freeman L: Loving Touches. Seattle, WA, Parenting Press, 1986

Gil DG: Violence Against Children: Physical Child Abuse in the United States. Cambridge, MA, Harvard University Press, 1973

Hart-Rossi J: Protect Your Child From Sexual Abuse. Seattle, WA, Parenting Press, 1984

Kempe CH, Kempe RS: Child Abuse. Cambridge, MA, Harvard University Press, 1978

Kluft RP: Childhood Antecedents of Multiple Personality Disorder. Washington, DC, American Psychiatric Press, 1986

MacFarlane K. Waterman J, Conerly S, et al.: Sexual Abuse of Young Children: Evaluation and Treatment. New York, Guilford Press, 1986

Malmquist P (guest ed): Child abuse. Psychiatr Ann 17:(4), 1987

McLaughlin L: Who's minding the children? Aegis: Magazine on Ending Violence Against Women 37:4–8, 1983

New York State College of Human Ecology for the Cornell Family Life Development Center: What's a Kid to Do About Child Abuse. 1987. Available from Cornell University Distribution Center, 7 Research Park, Ithaca, NY 14850 ($2.00)

Oates K (ed): Child Abuse: A Community Concern. New York, Brunner/Mazel, 1984

Oates K: Child Abuse and Neglect. What Happens Eventually? New York, Brunner/Mazel, 1985

Pelton LH (ed): The Social Context of Child Abuse and Neglect. New York, Human Sciences Press, 1981

Rogers GC, MD: Some poisonings are a form of child abuse. Inside U of L (University of Louisville) 4(5):5, 1984

Rome HP: Personal reflections: child abuse as a psychosocial issue. Psychiatr Ann 17:225, 228, 1987

Schetky DH, Benedek EP: Emerging Issues in Child Psychiatry And The Law. New York, Brunner/Mazel, 1985

Schostak J: Schooling in Violent Imagination. New York, Routledge and Kegan Paul, 1986

Walker CE, Bonner BL, Kaufman KL: The Physically and Sexually Abused Child. New York, Pergamon Press, 1987

Williams GJ, Money J (eds): Traumatic Abuse and Neglect of Children at Home. Baltimore, Johns Hopkins University Press, 1987

Wolfe DA: Child Abuse, Implications for Child Development and Psychopathology (Volume 10). Newbury Park, CA, Sage Publications, 1987

The Family and Violence

Bowlby J: Violence in the family as a disorder of the attachment and caregiving systems. Am J Psychoanal 44:9–27, 29–31, 1984

Breines W, Gordon L: The new scholarship on family

violence. Signs: Journal of Women in Culture and Society 8:490–531, 1983

Climie RC: The paradox of family violence. CMAJ 129:221, 1983

Coleman DH, Straus MA: Alcohol abuse and family violence. Paper presented at the meeting of the American Sociological Association, Boston, August 1979

Conte JR (ed): Journal of Interpersonal Violence. Concerned with the Study and Treatment of Victims and Perpetrators of Physical and Sexual Violence. Newbury Park, CA, Sage Publications, 1986

Davis D: Something Is Wrong at My House. Seattle, WA, Parenting Press, 1985

Dillon B: Providing peace at home. Baptist Peacemaker 7(2):1, 3, 1987

Dobash RE, Dobash RP: Wives: the 'appropriate' victims of marital violence. Victimology, An International Journal 2(3–4):426–442, 1978

Felson RB: Aggression and violence between siblings. Social Psychology 46:271–285, 1983

Finkelhor D, Gelles RJ, Hotaling GT, et al: The Dark Side of Families. Current Family Violence Research. Beverly Hills, CA, Sage Publications, 1983

Gelles RJ: The Family and Its Role in the Abuse of Children. Psychiatr Ann 17:229–232, 1987

Gelles RJ: Family Violence. Newbury Park, CA, Sage Library of Social Research, 1979

Gelles RJ: Family Violence (second edition). Newbury Park, CA, Sage Library of Social Research, 1987

Gelles RJ, Cornell CP: Intimate Violence in Families (Family Studies Text Series 2). Newbury Park, CA, Sage Library of Social Research, 1985

Grantham P: Perspective: the paradox of family violence. CMAJ 128:400–401, 1983

Hershorn M, Rosenbaum A: Children of marital violence: a closer look at the unintended victims. Am J Orthopsychiatry 55:260–266, 1985

Jouriles EN, O'Leary KD: Interspousal reliability of reports of marital violence. J Consult Clin Psychol 53:419–421, 1985

Justice B: Family violence. Tex Med 79(8):43–47, 1983

Justice B, Justice R: The Abusing Family. New York, Human Sciences Press, 1976

Kizer KW: Domestic violence: a EMS-targeted clinical condition in California. Ann Emerg Med 13:1082, 1984

Liddle HA (ed): Journal of Family Psychology (Journal of the Division of Family Psychology of the American Psychological Association, Division 42). Beverly Hills, CA, Sage Publications, 1987

Lystad M: Violence in the Home: Interdisciplinary Perspectives. New York, Brunner/Mazel, 1985

Medical, legal, and psychosocial aspects of violence in families. Bulletin of the American Academy of Psychiatry and the Law, Vol. 4, 1976

Rae-Grant Q: Family violence: myths, measures and mandates (Presidential Address). Can J Psychiatry 28:505–512, 1983

Russell GW: Violence In Intimate Relationships. Great Neck, NY, PMA Publishing Corporation, 1987

Schuman DC: Psychodynamics of exaggerated accusations: positive feedback in family systems. Psychiatr Ann 17:242–247, 1987

Schumm WR, Bollman SR, Jurich AP, et al.: Adolescent perspectives on family violence. J Soc Psychol 117:153–154, 1982

Straus MA: Leveling, civility, and violence in the family. Journal of Marriage and the Family 36:13–39, 1974

Straus MA, Gelles RJ, Steinmetz SK: Behind Closed Doors. Violence in the American Family. Garden City, NY, Anchor Books, Anchor Press/Doubleday, 1981

van Hasselt VB, Hersen M (eds): Journal of Family Violence. New York, Plenum Publishing, 1986

Wohl A, Kaufman B: Silent Screams and Hidden Cries: An

Interpretation of Artwork by Children from Violent Homes. New York, Brunner/Mazel, 1985

Wolfe DA, Jaffe P, Wilson SK, et al: Children of battered women: the relation of child behavior to family violence and maternal stress. J Consult Clin Psychol 53:657–665, 1985

Elder Abuse

Champlin L: The battered elderly. Geriatrics 37:115–121, 1982

Goodstein RK: Violence in the home: II. Battered parents and the battered elderly. Carrier Foundation Letter #126, June 1987, pp. 1–4

Hickey T, Douglass RL: Mistreatment of the elderly in the domestic setting: an exploratory study. Am J Public Health 71:500–507, 1981

Quinn MA, Tomita SK: The shame of elder abuse. Modern Maturity, October/November 1986, pp. 50–57

Quinn MA, Tomita SK: Elder Abuse and Neglect. New York, Springer Publishing, 1986

Rathbone ME, Voyles B: Case detection of abused elderly parents. Am J Psychiatry 139:189–192, 1982

Winter A: The shame of elder abuse. Modern Maturity, October/November 1986, pp. 50–57

Prevention

Edelstein BA, Michelson L (eds): Handbook of Prevention. New York, Plenum Publishing, 1986

Goodwin J: Family violence: principles of intervention and prevention. Hosp Community Psychiatry 36:1074–1079, 1986

Treatment Issues

Bolton FG, Bolton SR: Working With Violent Families, A Guide for Clinical and Legal Practitioners. Newbury Park, CA, Sage Publications, 1987

Daro D: Confronting Child Abuse: Research for Effective Program Design. New York, Free Press, 1988

Deschner JP: The Hitting Habit: Anger Control for Battering Couples. New York, Free Press, 1987

Emerge Collective: Organizing and Implementing Services for Men Who Batter. Boston, MA, Emerge, 1981

Eth S, Pynoos RS: Post-Traumatic Stress Disorder in Children. Washington, DC, American Psychiatric Press, 1985

Everstine D, Everstine L: People in Crisis: Strategic Therapeutic Interventions. New York, Brunner/Mazel, 1983

Figley CR (ed): Trauma and Its Wake: Vol. I. The Study and Treatment of Post-Traumatic Stress Disorder. New York, Brunner/Mazel, 1985

Figley CR (ed): Trauma and Its Wake: Vol. II. Traumatic Stress Theory, Research, Intervention. New York, Brunner/Mazel, 1986

Figley CR, McCubbin HI (eds): Coping with Catastrophe (Volume 2). New York, Brunner/Mazel, 1984

Garbarino J, Guttermann E, Seeley JW: The Psychologically Battered Child: Strategies for Identification, Assessment, and Intervention. San Francisco, Jossey-Bass, 1986

Goldberg WG: Domestic violence victims in the emergency department. JAMA 251:3259–3264, 1984

Gomes-Schwartz B, Horowitz JM, Sauzier M: Severity of Emotional Distress Among Sexually Abused Preschool, School-Age, and Adolescent Children. Hosp Community Psychiatry 36:503–508, 1985

Goodwin J: Family violence: principles of intervention and prevention. Hosp Community Psychiatry 36:1074 1079, 1986

Kelley JA: Treating Child-Abusive Families: Intervention Based on Skills Training Principles. New York, Plenum Press, 1983

Kirkland K: Assessment and treatment of family violence. J Fam Pract 14:713–718, 1982

Knopp RK: Domestic violence: a new priority for emergency medicine. Ann Emerg Med 13:636, 1984

Krajczar M, Lake W: Family violence: a perspective for health-care professionals. RNABC News 17:14–15, 1985

MacFarlane K, Waterman J, Conerly S, et al: Sexual Abuse of Young Children: Evaluation and Treatment. New York, Guilford Press, 1986

Martin JA: Neglected fathers: limitations in diagnostic and treatment resources for violent men. Child Abuse Negl 8:387–392, 1984

Nichols M: Family Therapy. New York, Brunner/Mazel, 1984

Oehlberg SM, Regan DO, Rudrauff ME, et al: A preliminary evaluation of parenting, depression, and violence profiles in methadone-maintained women. Natl Inst Drug Abuse Res Monogr Ser 34:380–386, 1981

Porter S: Recognizing and treating the victims of violence. Ohio State Med J 81:485–491, 1985

Quinsey VL (ed): The Prediction and Control of Violent Behavior. Journal of Interpersonal Violence 1(3), 1986

Raisanen MJ, Virkkunen M, Huttunen MO, et al.: Increased urinary excretion of bufotenin by violent offenders with paranoid symptoms and family violence. Lancet 2:700–701, 1984

Regan DO, Leifer B, Finnegan LP: Depression, self-concept, and violent experience in drug abusing women and their influence upon parenting effectiveness. Natl Inst Drug Abuse Res Monogr Ser 49:332, 1984

Renshaw DC: Evaluating suspected cases of child sexual abuse. Psychiatr Ann 17:262–270, 1987

Sgroi SM: A Handbook of Clinical Intervention in Child Sexual Abuse. Lexington, MA, Lexington Books, 1982

Stuart RB: Violent Behavior: Social Learning Approaches to Prediction, Management, Treatment. New York, Brunner/Mazel, 1981

Symonds M: Discussion of "Violence in the Family as a Disorder of the Attachment and Caregiving Systems." Am J Psychoanal 44:29–31, 1984

Turkat D, Buzzell V: The relationship between family violence and hospital recidivism. Hosp Community Psychiatry 34:552–553, 1983

van der Kolk BA: Psychological Trauma. Washington, DC, American Psychiatric Press, 1986

Viken RM: Family violence: aids to recognition. Postgrad Med 71:115–122, 1982

Yates A: Psychological damage associated with extreme eroticism in young children. Psychiatr Ann 17:257–261, 1987

Youth Violence

Goodstein RK: Violence in the Home: II. Battered Parents and the Battered Elderly. Carrier Foundation Letter #126, June 1987, pp. 1–4

Keith CR: The Aggressive Adolescent. New York, Free Press, 1987

Kratcoski PC: Youth violence directed toward significant others. J Adolesc 8:145–157, 1985

Rosenthal PA, Doherty MB: Psychodynamics of delinquent girls' rage and violence directed toward mother. Adolesc Psychiatry 12:281–289, 1985

Personal Violence

Russell DEH: Sexual Exploitation, Rape, Child Abuse and Workplace Harassment. Newbury Park, CA, Sage Library of Social Research, 1984

The Media

Eron LD: Parent-child interaction, television violence, and aggression of children. Am Psychol 37:197–211, 1982

Wharton R, Mandell F: Violence on television and imitative behavior: impact on parenting practices. Pediatrics 75:1120–1123, 1985

Wohl A, Kaufman B: Silent Screams and Hidden Cries: An Interpretation of Artwork by Children from Violent Homes. New York, Brunner/Mazel, 1985

Appendix 2

Contact Agencies

LEAH J. DICKSTEIN, M.D.

Appendix 2

Contact Agencies

Brother to Brother
1660 Broad Street
Providence, RI 02905
(401) 467-3710

CHILD, Inc.
Box 2604
Sioux City, IA 51106
(712) 948-3295

Coalition for Abused
  Women of Nassau County
P.O. Box 94
East Meadow, NY 11554
(516) 542-2594

Domestic Abuse Project
204 W. Franklin
Minneapolis, MN 55404
(612) 874-7063; and
206 W. Fourth Street
Room 21
Duluth, MN 55806
(218) 722-2781

Emerge
25 Huntington Avenue
Boston, MA 02116
(617) 547-9870

Men Stopping Violence,
  Inc. (MSV)
1020 Dekalb Avenue, N.E.
Atlanta, GA 30307
(404) 688-1376

National Center for Missing
  and Exploited Children
1835 K Street, N.W.
Suite 600
Washington, DC 20003
(800) 843-5678

National Coalition Against
  Domestic Violence
2401 Virginia Avenue, N.W.
Suite 306
Washington, DC 20037
(202) 293-8860

Parents Anonymous
The Kentucky Council on
  Child Abuse
240 Plaza Drive
Lexington, KY 40503
(606) 276-1299
In Kentucky, call
  (800) 432-9251

RAVEN
6665 Delmar
Room 302
St. Louis, MO 63130
(314) 725-6137

Spouse Abuse Centers
There are 700 centers in the
United States.
Look in your telephone
directory or contact
Al-Anon in your area.

Self-Administered Parent Stress Test for Your Patients

LEAH J. DICKSTEIN, M.D.

Appendix 3

Self-Administered Parent Stress Test for Your Patients

Do you as a parent have time just for yourself each week? Is one of your children two years old or younger? Do you talk to a friend or relative on the phone at least once a week? These are some of the questions of the Parent Stress Test, a questionnaire to help parents assess how stress and support balance out in their lives. The main points of the Parent Stress Test are:

1. Being a parent is not easy
2. All parents need support in raising their children

Every parent experiences multiple stresses in all phases of childrearing which are exacerbated by money worries, difficult relationships, and isolation. The Parent Stress Test underlines the importance of having a support system—neighbors, friends, and community activities. It is crucial for all parents to be able to reach out and talk with someone when the stresses of coping with their children begin to mount up. Parents Anonymous (1-800-882-1250) and the Parental Stress Line (1-800-632-8188) are two toll-free numbers parents can call for emotional support and for additional services.

The test was developed through the support of the Stone Center for Developmental Services and Studies at Wellesley College in consultation with Gerald T. Hotaling, Ph.D., of the

263

Family Research Laboratory of the University of New Hampshire.

Parent Stress Test

Being a parent is not easy. Sometimes stresses mount up, and the support that you need just is not there. Take the Parent Stress Test to see how "stress" and "support" balance out in your life. This test is not meant to be a professional evaluation, but it will give you a chance to look at some factors that can cause stress in your life.

Below are four sets of questions. Just follow the instructions and compute your total score at the end.

Section 1

First of all, here are some questions about yourself. Just answer "yes" or "no" in response to each question.

1. Are you under 30 years old? _____
2. Do you have more than two children? _____
3. Have you been married less than 10 years? _____
4. Is one of your children two years old or younger? _____

Section 2

This is a list of events that happen to many people. Answer "yes" or "no" for each question. Have these things happened to you in the past 12 months?

5. Trouble with other people at work or in the neighborhood. _____
6. Layoff or job loss. _____
7. Layoff or job loss of spouse or partner. _____
8. Death of someone close. _____
9. In-law troubles. _____
10. Serious sickness or injury. _____
11. Pregnancy or birth of a child. _____

12. Serious problem with health or behavior
    of a family member.   _____
13. New, serious financial problems.   _____
14. Increase in hours worked or job responsibilities.   _____
15. Increase in arguments with spouse/partner.   _____
16. Child involved in an illegal act or suspended
    or expelled from school.   _____
17. Hit by spouse/partner.   _____

Section 3

These next five statements are about your attitude and opinions. There are no right or wrong answers. Again, just indicate whether you agree ("yes") or disagree ("no") with each statement.

18. Children should know even before the age
    of two years what parents want them to do.   _____
19. I think preschoolers should know when parents
    are upset and try to be good at those times.   _____
20. Children will be glad later on that they had
    strict training.   _____
21. More parents should teach their children
    to always be loyal to them no matter what.   _____
22. Children should realize how much parents
    have to give up for them.   _____

Section 4

Below are some questions about people who may be supportive in your life. Answer "yes" or "no" for each question.

23. Have you lived in the same neighborhood
    for the last two years?   _____
24. Do you have a "best friend?"   _____
25. Are there at least three people you know
    whom you consider friends?   _____
26. Do you belong to at least one community

or church organization?   _____

27. Are there times during the week that you
    have just to yourself?   _____

28. Do you visit with relatives or do they visit
    you at least once every few weeks?   _____

29. Do you visit with friends or do they visit you
    at least once every few weeks?   _____

30. Are there times during the day when
    someone else takes care of your kids?   _____

31. Do you talk to friends or relatives on the phone
    at least once a week?   _____

32. Do you think talking to someone about
    personal or family problems is a good thing?   _____

33. Do you know of people or organizations
    in your community whom you could talk to
    about family or personal problems?   _____

Scoring:

1. First of all, add up your score for each section. For Sections
   1 and 2, add up the number of times you answered "yes."
   (Enter that number on the line at right) _____

2. Add up the total scores from Sections 1, 2 and 3. (Enter that
   number on the line at right) _____

3. For Section 4, give yourself 2 points for every "yes." (Enter
   that number on the line at right) _____

4. To find your overall score, subtract your score on Section 4
   from your total score on Sections 1, 2 and 3. (Enter that
   number on the line at right) _____

If your overall score is more than 0, you may want to consider
getting some support for you and your family. You may be under some stress and strain and getting some help could make
you feel more relaxed. Even if your score is less than 0, it is
always a good idea to talk to someone when you feel anxious
and stressed.

Reproduced with permission from the Stone Center.

65399

Family violence

HQ
809.3
.U5
F34
1989

	DATE DUE	DEC 1 8 2002	
MAR 1 2 1991	DEC 1 5 1995	DEC 1 8 2002	
APR - 9 1991	MAR 0 7 2000		
APR 1 7 1991	FEB 2 9 2000		
MAR 2 3 1992	APR 0 5 2000		
APR 2 1 1992	APR 0 5 2000		
NOV 3 0 1992	NOV 1 1 2000		
APR 0 5 1993	NOV 1 7 2000		
APR 2 2 1993	APR 2 6 2001		
nt	APR 2 5 2001		
	DEC 0 8 2001		
APR 1 9 1994	NOV 2 0 2001		
DEC 2 2 1995			